DARK CLOUDS
AND
SILVER LININGS

A COLLECTION OF WRITINGS BY SERVING BRITISH SERVICEMEN AND WOMEN, THEIR FAMILIES AND FRIENDS

COMPILED AND EDITED BY PRISCILLA DICKETTS

First published in 2010 by PSF Publications

Reprinted in 2011

Photographs©SSgt William Craig

Line drawings©James Fox

ISBN No: 13 - 978-0-9567445-0-0

The views expressed in all the poetry and prose in this book are solely those of the individuals who have contributed and not necessarily that of the publisher/editor or any other related organisation

Publisher/Editor: Priscilla Dicketts, Little Weald, Brenchley Road, Horsmonden, Kent, TN12 8DN
www.priscilladicketts.co.uk

Publishing Consultant: Zoe Meyer
www.zoesbooks.co.uk

Book Designer: Matt Swann
mattswanncreative.blogspot.com

Printed by TCPC - The Complete Product Company Limited
www.tcpc.co.uk

Front cover: Photo of Camp Bastion at dawn

CONTENTS

TALKING2MINDS

Post Traumatic Stress Disorder (PTSD) affects many of our veterans and service people. It can destroy lives. Not only for sufferers, entire families are adversely affected in the wake of symptoms displayed which can include, paranoia, unreliability, nightmares, flashbacks, lack of confidence and self medication. Most of us can leave our problems at work or at home. When you suffer with PTSD, it goes everywhere with you. Home to your partner and family; to picking a fight for no apparent reason; to panic attacks at the shopping centre; to sleepless nights with night terrors and flashbacks. Where does it end? Many of us have never contemplated or even thought of how we would cope with this kind of consistent anxiety.

What makes the Talking2Minds approach different is the unique and revolutionary way of treating the root cause of the condition and not the symptoms as do other therapies. With the Talking2minds approach it is not necessary to revisit traumatic events in any detail unlike other approaches which are trauma focussed. Many of the practitioners are ex-service personnel who have themselves suffered from PTSD and therefore have an intimate understanding of the condition – creating the "Veterans helping Veterans" ethos and where everyone is committed to supporting the families and partners that may be affected or suffering by proxy.

"I was in a dark place and the only light came from what I felt like a self-destruct button in front of my face. I was at rock bottom.. I spent only four days with Talking2Minds and by the end I had a feeling of calmness, clarity and positivity. I hadn't felt this way in 10 years. I left the programme with this feeling and it hasn't diminished. I have my life back and also a new network of friends that I know I can call on in any time of difficulty." **James, ex-Rifles**

www.talking2minds.co.uk

INTRODUCTION

This book would not have seen the light of day had it not been for a card sent to me after the death of our son in Afghanistan.

Thanks to Agnes's card and our subsequent friendship I found the most amazing poetry and prose about the pain of loss, loneliness, the fear of being alone and many other emotions written by families, friends and members of our Armed Forces.

We all have death in common which brings up fears of our own mortality. It is by acknowledging and reading these pieces that we begin to understand, in some tiny way, that we are all part of a whole and we all need to pull together. This is what I call the "silver lining" in every dark cloud. It has been my "silver lining" to be able to collect these poems, reflections and letters.

To acknowledge each one of you would be an impossible task. Moreover many of the pieces are by our troops and it would be irresponsible to mention names. You all know who you are! To all of you who have waived your copyright for this collection, my sincere thanks. For anyone who I have omitted to acknowledge, my sincere apologies. However special thanks go to James Fox for his drawings, to SSgt Will Craig for the photos and collation of both, to Zoe Meyer who has helped me through the layout maze and other hazards of publication and finally of course to Agnes Hunter. Lastly, thanks to my son Oliver, who has led my husband and I to many extraordinary places and to meeting many extraordinary people.

I hope that by reading these pages you will begin to understand a little more of the emotions felt by those at home and abroad.

It is important that we all show our support for the families left at home and for those who come back injured in mind or body, for these scars are the hardest to heal and they all need our love and support.

BE PROUD OF THEM!

Priscilla Dicketts
Kent, 2010

FOREWORD

In autumn 2006 the British Forces had been in Helmand, Afghanistan for five years. Every so often news would trickle through telling us what they were doing in this remote country, but on the whole most of what I was reading in the press was about the politics behind the deployment. The one story they never filed was far away from the political battlefield of Westminster. It was the account of the men and women sent into battle to fight the *War on Terror* on our behalf.

These are the real heroes so why weren't we hearing about them?

From that moment I set off to find out what it meant to be a British soldier fighting in Afghanistan on Britain's Frontline. I wanted to report the hardship the men and women suffered, the intensity of their daily pitched battles against the Taliban and, the very real danger they faced on the battlefield every single day of their tour. I needed to know how these men were coping so far away from their home and their loved ones who worried so much about them in the deadly heat of Helmand.

The next year I went to Afghanistan with my Father's old regiment, 1st Battalion The Royal Anglian Regiment. In that year our soldiers suffered the hardest fighting since the Second World War and Korea. When we broadcast the footage in early 2008 the viewing public were shocked at what our soldiers were doing to keep us safe.

A year on from my deployment to Helmand I remain strong in my belief that the story of the soldier is the most important one to be told.

That's why this book of poems is so important. It records for future generations the huge sacrifice our men and women have made, and continue to make, so we can live safer lives.

We must never forget them.

Ross Kemp
London 2008

GLOSSARY

IED	improvised explosive device
GMLRS	guided multi launch rocket systems
FOB	forward operating base
Hesco (walls)	prefab multi-cellular defence system
OPS	operations
The DC	district centre
EOD	explosive ordnance disposal
HLS	helicopter landing site
Det Inks	detachment clerk
Sangar	small fortification
ANA	Afghan National Army
Terp	Interpreter
BFBS	British Forces Broadcasting Service
Wadi	river bed

WHO ARE WE AND WHY?

WHO AM I?

Who am I?
I am your brother
I am your sister
I am your cousin
I am your son
I am your daughter
I am your friend

Who am I?
I am a Sailor
I ensure the world's waters are safe
I patrol and defend my Nation's coastline

Who am I?
I am an Airman
I ensure the world's sky is safe
I patrol and defend my Nation's airspace

Who am I?
I am a Marine
I am my nation's quick reaction force
I take the objective and hold it 'till relieved

Who am I?
I am a Soldier
I defend my nation from those who attack us
I take the objective and hold it 'till relieved

I don't ask you to understand
For I know you never truly will
The saying says that for those who have fought for it
Freedom has a taste the protected will never know

I do however ask that you respect
My life and what I did
Should I fall while defending my country
Don't use me for your own personal gain or agenda
Doing so cheapens my death and the ideals for which I died
I fight, kill and die for you
That you will never have to do what I have had to do

That you will never had to see what I have had to see
That you will never have to kill another as I have had to do

I do not enjoy killing
I do not enjoy watching my friends get wounded,
Maimed and killed
I sure as hell do not enjoy dying

I feel every single death of a military member
They are my brothers and sisters
Every time one of them dies I feel the loss

Try and remember to say thank you as you see me walk past
Understand when I say it's not necessary
I do what I do because I want to
Not because someone made me
I said I would and I will

Who am I?
I am your brother
I am your sister
I am your cousin
I am your son
I am your daughter
I am your friend

I am a member of the Armed Services

HOW DOES A SOLDIER FEEL FIGHTING A WAR?

How does a soldier feel fighting a war?
Does he always know what he is fighting for?
Maybe he knows but doesn't understand,
Why he is alone in a faraway land.

Like so many others he is there for a cause,
And like the rest he doesn't pause.
He has a job that he does well,
Even as his best friend beside him fell.

How does he feel when he hears the news,
Of violent protests from the ignorant few
His shame is great, the pain goes deep
He feels compassion for the dead at his feet.

Rioters can boast and carry signs,
About the war that has shook our time.
But when the call comes for them to go,
They burn their draft cards and make a show.

How can a soldier be proud of his land,
When these type of people make a stand?
How can we show him we are glad he is there,
Fighting for freedom and the ones who care?

War is unfair in any way of life,
And all involved must pay the price.
But the soldier is proud to keep us free,
Stop and think. Shouldn't you be?

THROUGH THE EYES OF A SOLDIER

If you look into the eyes of a soldier
Be they young, or be they old
And you could see what those eyes have seen
Your blood would soon run cold.

They've seen so much death and destruction
Caused by conflict through the years
And though they themselves won't tell you
These eyes have shed so many tears.
They've seen the broken bodies
Scattered all around
Killed by hidden devices
Buried in the ground.
And then there are the children
Left orphaned and alone
Their parents have been tortured and killed
By those they call their own.

They've seen armoured vehicles blown apart
Then heard the screams and shouts
Their brothers in arms trapped burning inside
While men try to get them out.
They've seen their fellow soldiers
Shot and cruelly killed
They want to stop but still carry on,
That's the discipline instilled.
There are no easy tasks that they've faced
Like patrolling on the streets
Bringing hearts and minds to innocents
Trying to bring them peace.

A soldier's eyes see many things
Some good, but far more are worse
And it's those visions that give them the nightmares
Like a never ending curse.
So when you look into the eyes of a soldier
And you see what they have seen
Will it ever make you wonder
What the point of war has been.

IDENTITY STOLEN

I used to have a name and my own style of dress
But now I have been changed to unify with the rest
We now all look the same, no way of standing out
My identity's been stolen, and of this I have no doubt

We have to march in squads, legs moving all the time
Being slightly different is looked at as a crime
There is no time for manners, all you here are shouts
My identity's been stolen, and of this I have no doubt

Your locker must be perfect, your clothes must look the part
Folding socks and ironing shirts must be mastered as an art
Everything must have its place, nothing will be left out
My identity's been stolen, and of this I have no doubt

They make you crawl through thick cold mud; shivers haunt your spine
Sometimes I whisper quietly "was this really a choice of mine?"
If you tried to complain to them they'd probably kick you out

My identity's been stolen, of this I have no doubt

I'll soon be at Gibraltar a few weeks to pass out
Looking up feeling good, new identity starts to sprout
I look back at my training, oh then it seemed so bad
But now I know I can stand tall and shout how I feel out loud

I'M PART OF THE BRITISH ARMY

I WORK AMONGST THE BEST

BETTER THAN HER

BETTER THAN HIM

JUST TYPICAL DAYS

In a far distant land brave soldiers awake
And rise from their beds before the dawn break

Bed spaces are tidied, ablutions are done
All before breakfast, their day's just begun

With body armour on, and helmets at hand
They go off for breakfast, in a tent in the sand

Reveille is next, the day's orders are heard
All listening in silence to the officer's words

In blistering heat some guard the base, standing proud
While others take supplies to the needy civilian crowds

Others sent out on operations, piled into bulldogs they're off
Maybe days of battle and almost no sleep, nothing but rations to scoff

Snipers, bombers, IED's, small arms fire no doubt
These are just a few things they face when patrolling out and about

They may go man down from illness or maybe injured or killed but
They still soldier on, for better or worse
Because of the discipline instilled

These are just typical days that they face, unlike you, or I,
Whilst most of us work in comfort and peace
They duck as missiles pass by

They carry out their jobs but cannot complain because that's what
They signed up to do and yet they receive so little respect for
Serving their country so true, so to all our service men and women
You deserve so much respect. Thank you.

HE AND YOU

You stay up for 16 hours
He stays up for days on end

You take a warm shower to help you wake up
He goes days or weeks without running water

You complain of a 'headache' and call in sick
He gets shot at as others are hit, and keeps moving forward

You put on your anti war don't support the troops shirt, and go meet
up with your friends
He still fights for your right to wear that shirt

You make sure your cell phone is in your pocket
He clutches the cross hanging on his chain next to his dog tags

You talk trash about your 'buddies' that aren't with you
He knows he may not see some of his buddies again

You walk down the beach, staring at all the pretty girls
He patrols the streets, searching for insurgents and terrorists

You complain about how hot it is
**He wears his heavy gear, not daring to take off his helmet to wipe
his brow**

You go out to lunch and complain because the restaurant got your
order wrong
He doesn't get to eat today

Your maid makes your bed and washes your clothes
**He wears the same things for weeks but makes sure his
weapons are clean**

You go to the shops and get your hair redone
He doesn't have time to brush his teeth today

You're angry because your class ran 5 minutes over
He's told he will be held over an extra 2 months

You call your girlfriend and set a date for tonight
He waits for the mail to see if there is a letter from home

You hug and kiss your girlfriend, like you do everyday
He holds his letter close and smells his love's perfume

You roll your eyes as a baby cries
**He gets a letter with pictures of his new child, and wonders if
they'll ever meet**

You criticise your government and say that war never solves anything
**He sees the innocent tortured and killed by their own people and
remembers why he is fighting**

You hear the jokes about the war, and make fun of men like him
He hears the gunfire, bombs and screams of the wounded

You see only what the media wants you to see
He sees the broken bodies lying around him

You are asked to go to the store by your parents. You don't
He does exactly what he is told even if it puts his life in danger

You stay at home and watch TV
He takes whatever time he is given to call, write home, sleep and eat

You crawl into your soft bed, with down pillows, and get comfortable
**He tries to sleep but gets woken by mortars and helicopters
all night long**

GET YOUR BACKBONE BACK

Look at you sitting there
Up in your ivory tower
Untrained, undisciplined
Which fool gave you the power?

You're making decisions
About these terrible wars
But do you actually know
What we are really fighting for?

You send our forces out to fight
Whilst we loved ones merely stand and wait
How many more lives must be sacrificed
Whilst you ponder on their fate?

Those men and women are fighting
For their country and their Queen
But would YOU put their shoes on
And tread where they have been?

On one hand you praise them
Then on the other you berate
You ought to make your minds up
No wonder this country's in such a state

Start listening to the masses
Stop pandering to the few
Forget this PC rubbish
Let common sense reign true
It's time this country's rulers
Stood behind our Union Jack
And made OUR Britain Great again
Get your backbone back!

FOR ALL OUR BRAVE LADS, THANKS

I heard that there were angels
Who walked amongst the damned
Who chose to live amongst them
To lend a helping hand

I heard they gave up Heaven
So they could live again
To bring support and comfort
Into the lives of men

I heard that their past memories
Were hidden from their sight
That they were birthed amongst us
By the giver of the light

I heard but did not quite believe
That these stories could be true
That was until I met an angel
Who took the form of you

WHEN YOU LOOK AT A SOLDIER

When you look at a soldier
What do you see?
Could someone out there
Please explain it to me.

What gives you the right
To treat them this way?
Here's a question for you
What have you done today?

You sit in your warm houses
With your family and chat
Let me tell you something
A soldiers life's not like that.

Their families don't see them
For months at a time
They are out in a war zone
They are on the front line.

They come home from battle
Don't know what to expect.
Isn't it time, Joe Public,
You gave them respect?

Next time you see a soldier
Don't know what to say
Just shake their hand
As they go on their way.

It's not too much to ask
It's not a lot to do
It's just saying, hey soldier
We do respect you.

SOLDIERS

They sleep on cots made for just one
Sometimes even with their boots on
They awake long before the sun
And work very hard to stay strong

Strong for themselves
Strong for their families
Strong for the country they serve
Strong for the flag that waves above

They work and train
In the heat, cold and rain
They sweat, they swear
Sometimes wondering why they are there

In the distance they hear gun fire
And watch the hawks fly over
They pray for their brothers
Their loved ones and themselves

And yet they go on
Doing their job
Determined to make proud
The ones that have passed on

They fight for justice
They serve for freedom
They cry for the fallen
And celebrate the day

These are our soldiers
Proud and strong
Serving flag and country
Away and at home

For the job they do
We need to give our support
So they know they are loved
From the depths of our hearts

OUR SPECIAL FORCES

I can say nothing, I endure the inane remarks of people with no knowledge or understanding of the world in which we live.

I suppose it is easy to ignore what is not in our own back yard. But it is here all around us in subtle and silent whispers. Dark flowing currents passing us by like shadows across a blue sky, invisible clouds of white, grey and dark thunderous storm clouds which become violent thunderstorms with sheet lightening.

It is not a question of blind panic, but of acceptance, understanding, compassion. Most of all of being positive, not letting negativity, hopelessness, fear and sadness take over!

This is why you came along, I am so proud of you all: the unsung heroes!

What you do and learn to do is the stuff of adventure stories, films, exciting imaginings. It is extraordinary; what you put into practice, even more so!

Yet we cannot shout your praises, we do not know how many wounded and, above all, how your combined efforts make our country and lives safe.

To all of you our thanks, how we would love to shout your names from the rooftops. But, your choice is the shadows, the faceless ones, calm cool and collected.

Bless you all.

THE GIFT OF A MOTHER'S LOVE

The soldier closed his eyes tight, his jaw bit hard to clench.
He reached across to his brother in arms who lay wounded in the trench.
His tears they remained guarded, his life flashed before his eyes.
No hope no freedom left for him until a voice came from the skies.
Son, this is your Mother, take heed and hear me well.
Remove your thoughts of sadness because in my heart you dwell.
Don't lay down your gun before you turn flight away and flee.
Stand up, be brave, be strong, be proud and face your enemy.
Son I'm right beside you reach out and take my hand
Take strength from the love I have for you
Feel my heartbeat in the sand.
Son I'm always with you my love so deep and true.
My arms made frail through age still have strength to carry you.
Son I'll never judge you when you face adversity.
Keep your tears in a trinket box and bring them home to me.
Son I'm right here waiting my arms are open wide
But until then hold your head up high for the men stood by your side.
The soldier raised his head up high his eyes glistened to the moon.
"Mother I feel you by my side and I promise I'll be home soon"

The soldier took his weapon and looked to the sky above.
"Thank God " he said to the cloudless night
"For the gift of a mother's love"

FAMILY FEELING

ARE YOU PROUD?

Do I miss him? Seems a silly question to ask.
How do I cope? I wonder at times.
Do I feel alone? In a room full of people.
And yet the one question I am never asked is…am I proud?
Am I proud? With every twinkle of hope and despair,
I wish you could see how much I care.
It pains me to know there are those, who don't understand,
If only they knew their lives are in your hands.
It amazes me the things you do everyday,
It is so overwhelming; I guess what I'm trying to say,
I love you and you make me so proud, every single day.

INSPIRED BY YOU, CREATED BY ME, WITH LOVE TO MY BOY!

My baby boy, all grown up
Now a man and off to war
It doesn't seem that long ago
You were crawling on the floor.

My first born son, now so tall
Not a baby any more
I'd wished for you a peaceful world
Not one full of hate and war.

TODAY I READ A STORY

In the papers about a lad who saved his mate's life in Afghan by dodging bullets during an ambush to give medical aid to his mate who was wounded. He then "hauled" his 15 stone pal on to his shoulders and carried him through the sweltering heat back to camp. Camp was 90 minutes away and he carried him all the way.

My lad is going to Kosovo at the end of the month. He just turned up out of the blue last night, smiling and happy because he had just passed his driving test yesterday morning. His last leave before active service.

I know he survived Iraq and Kosovo is a bit volatile but not as bad as Afghan, (he's due there next year) and I'll always worry a little when he is in a war zone. But, I think I will worry a little less now because I know he will be amongst friends. I know and he knows that any of his mates would do the same for him as the lad in the paper, and he would do it for them. He won't be alone and scared if the worse happens, his mates will move Heaven and Earth to get him to safety.

I had tears in my eyes reading the story; but not sad tears. They were tears of pride and admiration for all our lads. I know its hard for all of us waiting at home and yet I felt today, that I shouldn't let my tears blind me to the virtue and heroism that is in the world.

Tears are like rain clouds, when you are all cried out there are no more clouds and all you are left with are blue skies. My boy is my sunshine. My tears are the rain, and we all know what happens when it rains on a sunny day.

You get a Rainbow.

BROTHER OF MINE

Each day I look out of my window
I think I see him so I stare
I see his face among the trees
But brother mine you're not there

I see the news
I think of you
We hold our chins up
To stay from the blue

I see my mum
Scared so much
I see her tears so full of care
But brother mine
Brother mine, you're not there

I think of you
When I'm trying to sleep
Worrying about you
Awake I keep

I see your friends
Hanging around the fair
They ask how you are
But brother of mine you're not there

I sit in your room when I'm all alone
Thinking of the fun it used to be
Now you're not here the feeling is low
Brother of mine we love you more than
You'll ever know

REPLY TO MY BROTHER

In the desert light
That's where you'll find me
Holding up the fire fight
So that you are free

On a desert road
That's where you'll find me
Collapsing under a heavy load
So that you are free

Kicking down a door
That's where you'll find me
Because out here we are the law
So that you are free

In the desert storm
That's where you'll find me
I think of you to keep me warm
Helping you to be free

In the scalding day
That's where you'll find me
Remember I'm not here to stay
Remember that you're free

Under the bright light moon
That's where you'll find me
Brother I'll be home soon
Then we'll both be free.

MUST NOT QUIT

When things go wrong as they sometimes will
When the road you're trudging seems all uphill
When funds are low and the debts are high
And you want to smile but you have to sigh

When care is pressing you down a bit
Rest if you must, but don't you quit

Life is **** with it's twists and turns
As every one of us sometimes learns
And many a person turns about
When they might have won, had they stuck it out

Don't give up though the pace seems slow
You may succeed with another blow
Often strugglers have given up
When you might have captured the victors cup
And you learned too late when the night came down
How close you were to the golden crown

Success is failure turned inside out
The silver tint of the cloud of doubt

So stick to the fight when you're hardest hit
It's when things seem worse that you
MUST NOT QUIT

YOU WERE NOT THERE

Last night I dreamed
I searched the tired faces
Of the soldiers as they marched
You were not there.
They marched in file
In unit and battalion
You were not there.
Through a sea of camouflage
Desert khaki, dress blues and kilts
You were not there.
I asked the stragglers
Making up the rear
Have you seen my boy?
He was with us, answered one
Looking wistfully behind
You were not there.

This morning on the radio
I heard 'another soldier killed'
You were not he.

Last night in my dream
I searched through
The ranks of the dead.

Oh what joy to find
You were not there.

A FATHER'S PRAYER

Goodbye for now, forgive my tears
They come from knowing you all these years
My sadness is me missing you
Thinking what you'll be going through

Goodbye, for now, but not too long
I promise that I will be strong
I promise I'll live my life and try to smile
Though you'll be in my heart all the while

Goodbye for now, my proud brave son
I picture you neither at war nor holding a gun
The only visions I have in my mind
Is of a boy, loving, gentle and kind

Goodbye, for now, we'll pray for you
My son that's all that we can do
We'll pray and hope for every one
For every father, brother, lover and son

Goodbye, for now you'll soon be back
To light up our lives with your wonderful laugh
Come back safe, I don't care how
Just come back to us, so goodbye, for now.

DO YOU KNOW WHAT IT'S LIKE?

Do know what it's like, do you know?
To have to say goodbye to your Son
When your heart is breaking and he's
Over there making what they hope will
Be a better life for some.

Do you care what we feel, do you care?
You seem to just look at me and stare
My Son is only eighteen, he says he is
Living the dream.
Would you come shake his hand, would you dare?

Would you swap life with me, hey you there.
Let me close my eyes with not a care.
Let me sleep at night not wake up with a fright
And cry out "Lord please keep him safe there"

Do you know what its like, do you know?
To be so very PROUD of your Son.

ISOLATED PARENT

My son is 18 and serving abroad. He is due home in a few days for R&R and I'm so scared. He's been up and down like most of the lads, been injured and seen the true horrors of this war. There have been many sleepless nights and tears on my part.

He has said he needs to talk to me and get things off his chest; things he has already told me have horrified me. I'm worried I won't have the words for him, the right words I mean. I'm getting myself in a state. I know that the things he's going to talk about will be heartbreaking. You don't expect a child of yours to see such things. I will of course listen and very probably cry with him.

I also know that at this time I will feel more isolated as a mum than ever, as I try to come to terms with what he has been through and worry how it will affect him mentally. I know it sounds selfish "how I will come to terms with things", but as mums we protect our children all we can and when it's out of our hands we have to learn to deal with it, and that's the hardest thing.

After he was injured I spoke to welfare, they said you do understand he's going to come back a very different boy? He will no longer be a boy, but very grown up. I thought I'd seen that the day he passed out, I guess I didn't. How awful I sound, I'm scared of seeing my own son!

What a way to 'grow up'.

I pick him up from the airport in a few days.

REPLY FROM ANOTHER ISOLATED PARENT

Listen, first, you are not in any way selfish for feeling as you do, far from it!

You are a loving caring mum who's heart is broken for her boy, knowing he's been through all that, and wondering how you can help him, and what to expect when you see him again.

Guess what, I have a confession to make.... I was just as scared to see my son when he was on R&R for 13 days after Christmas. I just didn't know how he would be or what he would tell me. It was all unknown territory, and made worse by the fact that I felt so GUILTY for even thinking that, and I felt I couldn't possibly tell any one.... How could I explain that I was scared of seeing my own son? (the tears have started again as I write this). Of course, I was DESPERATE to see him and hug him and see for myself he was ok (at least physically) but that fear was there all the same. How will he be? What if I don't know what to say to him? Will he be really different? Moody? What? I just didn't know.

Well, the answer was that he was himself, yet different, if you can understand me. More mature, definitely (and I thought he was mature for his age, well he was!) But he was definitely moodier and could be quite cutting at times reducing me to tears. We ended up having a good heart to heart one day (after I started crying my eyes out in MacDonalds of all places!) and we told each other how we felt and the various reasons why we both found it hard. After that he said he felt better for having cleared the air and that we both understood each others feelings.

He was noticeably happier after this, and we spent the last few days of his leave doing lovely things together and having a laugh. I was then heartbroken when he had to go back, but that's a whole other story....

The thing is, as a mum, you are the centre of your child's universe for a very long time, and its such an intense relationship. Then they grow and make their own way in the world, and the relationship changes, but that bond is unbreakable.

When he first came home, almost as soon as he set foot in the door he was telling us things that made my hair curl! It was like he couldn't stop himself talking at 100 mph, everything pouring out at once.

Then he met up with some Army mates and went living it up, then he became morose, snappy, impatient – in fact his moods were so mercurial I didn't know where I was. (Manic laughter one day and the next he would bite your head off). His dad couldn't see the problem, but, as I said, it's the mum who gets all the emotions and picks up on every little thing.

One day he went out and when he came back I had to tell him his Battalion had lost a lad, and that was so hard to do. I had debated not telling him, but thought he will find out anyway and might be annoyed with me for not telling him sooner. His first reaction was, "who is it?" it better not be (he named his best mate). Then he got a call from someone else on leave and found out who it was. That was hard for him, and I was crying so much for the Sgt who had lost his life, for his fiancée, for his family, and for the fact that my 18 year old son was having to come to terms with another death like this. He had already been involved in Repatriation Ceremonies for 4 colleagues.

So what I am trying to say here is that you won't know how either you or your son will be until he gets home, and that won't be easy. **But you will get through it, I promise**

Don't be afraid of crying in front of him, don't be afraid if he wants to cry and does cry in front of you – it all helps to come to terms with everything.

Your lad has a lot to tell you and you will need to be that shoulder to cry on and those listening ears, not to mention the sounding-board, advocate and general helper and comforter…as I said, it won't be easy – there will be good days and bad. Just remember you're his mum and no one else can be there for him and love him the way you do. So, believe in yourself and your own instincts and knowledge of your boy, you will get through, and that bond will be even stronger. And…..

Make sure that he, you and the family get all the support the Army has to offer.

LOOK WELL TO THIS DAY

Look well to this day
For it is life
The very best of life
In its brief course lie all
The realities and truths of existence
The joy of growth
The splendour of action
The glory of power
For yesterday is but a memory
And tomorrow is only a vision
But today if well lived makes
Every yesterday a memory of happiness
And every tomorrow a vision of hope
Look well, therefore, to this day

(Ancient Sanskrit poem)

WELCOME HOME

My arms are waiting to hold you
My heart is bursting with pride
I'm longing for the day when you walk in the door
And my son, you are back by my side.

My shoulders are here for you to lean on
My ears will hear what you don't tell
Be assured my precious much loved son
I know that you have been going through hell

You will be safe in the arms of your loved ones
Be assured we will not let you fall
Don't care if it's morning or night time
All it takes is for you to call.

So there's no need to pretend with your mum, son
I know you only too well
Everyday that you've been protecting the people
I, too, have been going through hell.

LETTERS

He sits in his tent In the dark of night writing a letter
With only a torch to light the paper that is important
So the pen he does hold tight in his grasp
So the words unfold

She sits at the table with pen and paper to hand
To write to her son who is out in the sand
She writes and she writes oh how the pages do fill
Without letting him know his mum feels constantly ill

He finishes his letter with that special phrase
'I Love You All' his mind is in a haze

Her letter is finished she writes 'Love You Sweetheart'
And all of the time she is falling apart

These two letters are posted and unknowingly pass in the sky
Thousands of miles up but very close by

He opens his letter with a smile on his face
All agony of pain, nobody sees a trace

She reads his letter with tears in her eyes
And with every word there are painful sighs

These two letters mean more than any others say
So locked in their hearts each word will stay.

FOR ALL PARENTS OF SOLDIERS

He is gentle, kind and caring,
A giant amongst men,
He cares, he gives, and he loves
He's gone to war!

Jeans and T-shirt
That's my son
Full of life
Full of fun
He's gone to war!

His smile is oh so gentle
His eyes are full of love
Protect and keep him safe
I pray to God above
He's gone to war!

Combats, helmet and a gun
Is that soldier really my son?
Gone to serve and protect
Hearing the cries for help
He's gone to war!

I look beyond the battle dress
Deep into his eyes
Full of laughter, love and care
Yes, that is my son in there!
He's gone to war!

Miles apart but still I will stand
By your side, I will hold your hand
I love you too much to let you go
We have gone to war!

MISSING OUR SOLDIERS

The time has come for you to go
To that place that we all know
Exchanging words is hard to do
Don't seem enough saying our love's so true
Not many people understand our plight
As we see you leave upon that flight
It gives loved ones at home the blues
Not knowing, except for Sky news

Parcels and letters, writing has begun
For a husband, father, brother, lover or son
Telling how proud we are of you
And many other words to help you through
Waiting here for news that you are well
Hoping, praying that all is swell

A letter returns with the words we need
A rush to open it and begin to read
Letting us know you miss us as we do you
You're feeling lonely, though busy too
We eagerly wait close by the phone
For your 30min gap to call home
Remember while serving in Iraq or Afghan
That you are all someone's very special woman or man
Looking forward for your return
For your hugs and kisses we do yearn

Loving a soldier is hard to do
But always we will wait for you
To see your smile or hold your hand
When you return to your homeland
If things get bad while you're away
Think of words that we would say
Keep yourself safe and keep in your mind
We all love you, those left here behind
Support our troops while they are serving
They need us as to come home safe they are yearning
All that I have left to say is....
I'm missing you my soldier in every way

LONELINESS

Whenever the feeling of loneliness
Creeps into your heavy heart
And makes you weep
Just close your eyes
And I am there
To soothe your brow
And show you I care

For you see my love
The day you went away
I was also deployed
That very same day

I walk each step with you
Through the miles of sand
Like when you were little
I still hold your hand

The reason I can do all this
Is spiritually we are never apart
Because not only did you pack your kit
You packed my love and heart in it

LET ME TAKE YOU ON A JOURNEY

Let me take you on a journey that is long and winding
And at the end of it
I promise your nerves will be grinding

You won't need a seat belt, a ticket or pass
Because taking this journey
There is no first class

The first thing you'll feel is the utter dread
With "I'm being deployed"
Words you never want said

At some point in our journey horrible storms will brew
All I can say is
There'll be more than a few

On very rare days the sun will come out
You've heard from a loved one
It's got rid of your doubt

We carry on now at a very slow pace
Like a weary worn traveller
It's etched on your face

Oh dear me you've gone off your food
What, you didn't realize
The public could be so nasty and rude

So now you are in sight of the end
Don't get excited
There's bound to be a twist and a bend

Sorry for the delay in getting you back
I just hope understanding
You now will not lack

Thank you for traveling sorry it's been so fraught
I sit here broken hearted
My son you see has just departed off to war in Iraq
Without the proper kit upon his back

Dear Mr Blair do you care?
Stood in your life of vanity fair
You chose to send them into this hell
The least you could do was equip them well

The worry and stress we have to endure
For a soldier's family there is no cure
No peace of mind or goodwill
Even the public wish them ill

What's happened to our country
What's happened to our pride
Why do I have to walk this path
My pride I'm told to hide

I will tell you something
This I shall not do
For I'm a soldier's mum
And son I'm bloody proud of you

As I count the days, hear me lord I do pray please
Please dear God let him return
To the waiting arms of this soldiers mum

It will be thanks to you, and not to Blair
Because one things for sure
He doesn't care
Shame on you our Mr. Blair

HOW DO YOU DEAL WITH PREPARING FOR DEPLOYMENT?

It was hard for us both at times as our son went off to Iraq and then six months later Afghan – the worse time of our lives.

Life has to go on but it's not the same you think about, and worry about, them each and every day and they are never out of your mind.

Not a lot helped me, not at first anyway. Then I started card making and as silly as it sounds it did help a little!

The hard bit prior to the deployment is while you have them at home and then the leaving is horrendous.

Once they are there and settled in and you hear from them, you feel just a little better – just a little. The winter nights were hard and lonely and you do constantly pine for them.

Yes, work helps – thank God I work and have a wonderful job. I often talk to the children about my son and show his beautiful photograph to them. This helps me a lot.

Joining a website helped so much – it's just untrue – I have been a member now for almost 18 months and I have started a book club forum – things like this do help – getting involved and talking to others.

I love books and reading so this helps a lot too – you have to find things to keep your mind occupied and although at the start it is hard and you think you will never cope, you do.

When you start to pine turn to something you love doing and DO IT.

Hope this helps…. We have to go through it all again soon and I just hope I cope as well this time too.

DEAR LORD

Every single evening as I'm lying here in bed
This tiny prayer keeps running through my head

God bless all my family wherever they may be
Keep them warm and safe from harm
For they're so close to me

And God, there is one more thing I wish that you could do,
Hope you don't mind,
Please bless my computer too

Now I know that it's unusual to bless a motherboard
But, listen, just a second, while I explain it to you Lord

You see that little metal box holds more than odds and ends
Inside those small compartments
Rest so many of my friends

I know so much about them by the kindness that they give
And this little scrap of metal
Takes me in to where they live

By faith is how I know them much the same as you
We share in what life brings us
And from that our friendship grew

Please take an extra minute from your duties up above
To bless those in my address book
That's filled with so much love

Wherever else this prayer may reach to each and every friend
Bless each email inbox
And each person who hits "send"

When you update your heaven on your own great CD-ROM
Bless everyone who says this prayer
Sent up to GOD.COM

REFLECTION

REMEMBRANCE 1

Today when handing out posters in my town a shopkeeper said to me "they do so much and we don't thank them. We don't look after them".

I was inspired to write:

You are brave
You are the reason I am free
You work so hard and never complain
You are thousands of miles away
You keep me and my family safe
You are the protector of everything I call 'home'
You are a son
You are a daughter
YOU ARE A SOLDIER

REMEMBRANCE 2

Wear your poppy
Wear it with pride
Remember those who fought and died
They heeded the call and went to war
For many brave soldiers
Life was no more
Just two minutes does not seem to suffice
To remember them
For their sacrifice

TOMORROW'S VETERAN

When I am old
With my medals on my chest
Will you be grateful
That I did my very best?

When I am old
Will these words still haunt me
'We shouldn't have been there'
Even though I helped keep you free

When I am old
And tears for my comrades fall
Will any of you understand
Side by side we stood, proud and tall

When I am old
Will you forget about me
Because if today you don't acknowledge us
Then tomorrow, our parades you won't want to see.

MEMORIES

Memories last longer than dreams,
Of this you can be sure
For when you lose someone you love
You leave ajar a door

From time to time you will look inside
Where you will see a book
It's called the book of memories
Just sit and take a look.

As you turn the pages one by one
Thinking of days gone by
You will recall such memories
That makes you feel warm inside.

Everyone's life is like a book
A beginning, middle, and end
But the book that we call memories
Will be read time and time again.

A DIFFERENT MEMORY

No spark of life in my eyes. I am not home, my body is here but my mind is with the lads. I've got to go back soon and I cannot afford to put the barriers down. My body is taking a break but my heart and mind is back with the lads.

IN SILENT MIND YOU GO

When you are home son I will know this
In my heart, I will know
For you are here but you are lost
And in silent mind you go

I reach out to you but you do not feel
No emotions there to show
For you are here but you are lost
So in silent mind you go

The part you left in that faraway place
Continues to plague and grow
For you are here but you are lost
As in silent mind you go

I will wait for you to return
With outstretched arms and tears will flow
While you are here but you are lost
And in silent mind you go

For I see the pain that lives within you
When in silent mind you go
And when you are truly home again
Son, in your own heart you will know

Dream sweet dreams not of war and pain
For when you dream of these things there is no gain
For your mind is etched with death and all that lies before
And you are lost in limbo in destruction bombs and war
You have lived to fight again and all that you have seen
Will live with you always and mould your life

YOU ARE IN MY HEART

You are in my heart
Even when we are apart
You are in my waking day
You are in the words I say

You are in the sky above
In my unceasing love
You are in the winds that blow
You are in my tears that flow

You are in my unending pride
I walk always by your side
Unseen and miles away
I'm with you every step of the way

When the road seems too hard to travel
Reach for my hand I will guide you
Through the pain and gentle rains that fall
I will help you to recall
That carefree life that once was had
When you were just a little lad
See you are my blood and of my bones
So my darling son you will never be alone.

DEPLOYMENT

Other things may change us, but we start and end with family - *Anthony Brandt.* Before he went, little was I to know how 'this thing' would change me in a way that I could barely recognize myself.

It finally came, the news I had been dreading. He told me the date so that it meant it was for real. He was going to the sandy place, and there wasn't anything that anyone could do about it. I couldn't write him an excuse letter as I had done when he couldn't be bothered to do P.E all those years ago. I couldn't write "Dear Sgt Major, please excuse him from the war as his kit is in the wash". Now that wouldn't wash. The more you wish that time would stand still it has a habit of free-falling you to your destiny and there is not a damned thing you can do about it except wait for the thud.

My thud came soon enough. I knew it would but prayed it wouldn't. He came to see me before he went. I could see the fear he had and how he desperately clung to the fact that we would see each other again, although looking back I could tell he was giving everything the final look over just in case this wasn't to be. We cried, or I cried, floods. I had tried to be so brave as I needed him to know I was 100% behind him, but in the end I succumbed to the fear of knowing that as he was looking around maybe for the very last time, that I was also looking at him maybe for the very last time. You can never know how that feels if you have never been there and I never want to be there again. We hugged and he told me to be brave for him and then he left. He had gone and there was nothing of him left where he had stood. I took the rosebud from the bunch of flowers he had brought me. It was yellow and tinged with deep red on the very end of the petals. I placed it draped over my very favorite picture of him, man in action! It stayed there till he came home and made me wake up again.

I called them Groundhog days. The days where, on arising from restless sleep, this heavy dread settled on me and I wore that shroud every day for half a year. Half a whole year! 'Don't worry the time will pass quickly' they said, 'he'll be back in no time' they said. But it didn't and he wasn't.

How can you live each day knowing that it may be his last? That if it ever was would I feel it in my heart before they told me, would they tell me, what if they couldn't find me because I was not where they could find me? All these things you think about and you mould your life, such as it is, around these things.

Now, looking back I realise that there was nothing in this world that could have prepared me for what lay ahead. I could say in hindsight that I should have been stronger, but of course they say hindsight is a wonderful thing!

We have to be strong for him, for the boy, so he doesn't worry about us and end up not devoting his thoughts to what lay ahead for him. Especially when the other one was in his dark place. We did it, we managed that one or other helped him keep his eye on the ball in the sandy place.

I always imagine that when they got off the plane they realised they had landed in hell, and of course they had. Who wanted him to be there, not us, not them, and certainly not him, so why was he?

Of course the phone calls were very short as time and cost did not allow the luxury of small talk. Every conversation was strained by the things that we couldn't say and of course wanted to so desperately. Can't be soft now as he needs to be strong, he is a soldier at war, no he is just our boy, as he always will be forever and always.

His spirit at times was non-existent and even his voice was not his own. Often he could barely speak the words, like he was very drunk, although never a drop went through him till home. Every message he left is still on the answer phone, like a compendium of his mindset, today I listen to them and my heart aches for the times that he reached out for me but I was not here to pick up the phone as I was having my own non existent life, like him.

Life was certainly very strange while he was gone, everything I had done and believed in stopped. The tears came of course, usually at the most inopportune moments, in full view of strangers, who must have thought I had completely lost it and of course I had. I do remember my husband, with deep concern saying I would make myself poorly if I carried on crying like this, but home was the only place I could do this without an audience. I carried on with the crying because it was something I needed to do, probably more user friendly than self harm eh? The bath was my haven, there I could do what I wanted as loudly as

I wanted while the water ran over my face. In the end he just said to get through it however I could, and I did, he never confronted the subject of how I would make myself poorly again, as I think he realized I was going to be very poorly for a very long time.

I do give my utmost thanks to him during this time as he never challenged the fact that the house was a tip, no meals made and my constant thirst to know what was happening every minute of every day in the sandy place. Sleep came via nightcaps to which I became very partial to, even the taste of the spirit as it burnt my throat made me realize that it was the only thing I had physically felt that day. Of course then I had my ritual which I had to do every night, alongside holding the rank slide underneath my pillow. The same words and thoughts each night and woe betide if I got a word or thought wrong as I had to redo it all from the very beginning, just in case I had left a gap where the evil could get in to him.

You are my son and I love you

Wherever you are and what ever you do I am thinking of you.

I place this shield around you to protect you from those who wish to do harm to you.

3 times with the right hand, his face on starting with the lower left leg, to the top of the head and down the other side, that's 6 times in all. Rather hard to concentrate with silent words and tracing around him in your mind. Still if I went wrong all had to start again, to get it perfect you see!

Your dear departed family are with you and the light they form around you will guide you and protect you from those who wish to do you harm.

Your number one angel is there to ease your troubled mind by sleep and to help in dark to enable you to walk safely in light.

Then and only then when it was perfect would I be able to think about trying to go into the coma called sleep, before another Groundhog Day began.

I had a place where I was at one with him on my route to work each day, where the sunrise hit suburbia, and it would fill me with a beautiful warm feeling to know that he would be looking at the same sun as I was gazing at. He would see it every morning before me and I knew that he had looked at it and it made me feel at peace as though we had something in common for that day. Although our terrain was certainly worlds apart, that ball of light was something which we shared.

Looking back it makes me smile to think that I would always ask him, in my very British mum way what the weather was like over there, to which he once answered 'well, half the camp is waterlogged and there's snow covering the other half, mum, what do you think the weathers like? – we're in the bloody desert!!!!' Despite his one and only cheeky outburst, I still continued to ask every time about the weather and I'm sure he found it easier just to give me the answer I required without the flippancy.

We all get through 'this thing' in our own way and my way was to always feel in control of what I was able to do. I needed to know what had happened in that sandy place and I know that many people get through their 'thing' by doing exactly the opposite, by not constantly scouring the newspapers or watching the news. I did try this but it wasn't for me and sometimes I wish just for one day I could have turned it all off. But I couldn't. It became an obsession even in my working day to make sure I was able to catch the hourly news in case something had happened and I didn't know about it.

When the news came that one of our boys had been lost it would fill me with such fear that if it was my boy I wouldn't be in the place where they would be able to contact me. I think it was one of the most intense feelings throughout the time and one which I'm sure so many of us will identify with. The feeling of fear, sheer panic and dread and then the prayers, please God let it not be my boy, and when it wasn't that split second relief followed by the feeling of such pain for the lovely mother of that lovely boy who had been lost that sad day. There were many of those sad days and I often found myself screaming at the top of my voice 'no more, no more, please no more!' but of course there were more and I will always remember those feelings of being helpless to prevent them.

I think to say I was probably bordering on some kind of OCD would be pretty bang on, also probably tinged with a kind of madness that although no one ever spoke to me about, they all skirted round the subject unwilling to rock the already rocky boat that was my mood swings. I mean how could they know how I felt when I didn't even know myself what I was feeling, if anything. One day so low that I could not feel anything until I got so fed up with this pathetic me. Then the other side of me, the anger at allowing myself to stop fighting when I needed to be strong for him and all around me. After all they all wanted to know how he is, what is he doing. I became the newscaster, telling them all the same thing, as if reading a carefully prepared script.

Usually everyone looks forward to summer, as I have always done in the past, but I wasn't this time. I was eagerly awaiting the cold days to come, and the nights to draw in. I remember years ago my dad used to say "it won't always be dark at 6 o'clock lass" when I had any worries and couldn't see my way out of them and I have always remembered that saying. This time I was praying for the time it really would be dark at 6 'clock as that would mean that the boy would be here with us again, where he belonged and where we all needed him to be. I along with all the other loved ones left at home would be the only ones waiting to welcome the cold and dark of autumn.

Finally that autumn day did come, and it was not dark when he flew home to us, it was a perfect summer blue sky, cloudless except for the white trails of many other homeward bound souls. I remember looking up and thinking it's all over now. How long I had waited for that day and to look up in that blue atmosphere and know my boy was in it was the most emotional moment I have felt, it was sadness and happiness in equal quantities.

He is back amongst us now, and there have been many, many times when I still relive those painful Groundhog days and I feel like I have been battle scarred by proxy, not there, but lived it, as if.

I lived the pain and I still do, but slowly I am starting to realize that although I did live it, more importantly I lived through it.

I have come to think of our lives as being like an antique piece of furniture. We accumulate many light scratches and some deep grooves, but those are the pieces you will look at and see character in and know that it has seen life in its time.

I WONDER IF YOU EVER KNEW

In this world
That is seldom kind
Think of those far away
And those left behind

In sweltering heat
And freezing cold
They mourn the young;
That will never grow old.

We stare at a screen
Dreading words spoken
That in one split second
Can leave our world broken

Dreading a ringing phone
Or knock at the door
And just as I think
'I can't take anymore'

You're back and you're safe
You didn't leave me behind
You're back in my world
That is so seldom kind

I wonder if you ever knew
That for all that time
While you were fighting Our War
I was fighting mine

RUBY RED FALLING

The knife hovers,
Suspended in the morning air.
The shaft rests comfortably in your hand.
Sunlight glints on steel
As ruby red falls, drop, by drop.
Your face is a mask.
No words are spoken,
For what could be said.

The light in your eyes has dimmed.
I watch you, retrace your thoughts,
Lowering the knife, you spread
Strawberry jam, on your toast,
And I will never ask,
And you will never tell,
If death stalks your dreams,
And is there blood on your hands.

I MISS YOU SO MUCH

I'm far away and worlds apart
From the beautiful girl who has my heart
She makes me smile on my darkest days
And has changed my life in so many ways
Beautiful memories of her soft kiss
Her soft voice that I always miss
I hope these lonely days fly by
So I can wipe the tears from her eyes
Longing for the day she becomes my wife
Who I will love and respect for the rest of my life.

JUST ANOTHER DAY

My alarm clock rings in the depth of my dreams
The noise far away or so it seems
Before opening my eyes I reach out for you
To cuddle you close as I always do

But you are not there, you've gone far away
I remember this at the start of each day
I stretch and I yawn as I start to rise
Blinking the tears away from my eyes

I hurry downstairs, put a cross on my chart
Kiss the picture of the man who's stolen my heart
I think of you as I drink my tea
Knowing this separation has to be

You've not left by choice; you've a job to do
And I hope you know I'm so proud of you
I leave the house to go to work too
And all through the day my thoughts turn to you

You're always there in my mind and my heart
So close to me even though we're apart
I get through the day and do what I must
Manage to smile but only just

When I get home I look to see
If the postie has brought a letter for me
From the man I adore who's so far away
Sometimes there is one but not today

I switch on my lap top and watch the time
And wait until you can come on line
And suddenly your there and my heart is glad

And all of a sudden the day's not that bad

You make me smile as we say hi
Now its tears of joy that flood my eyes
For you're safe and sound and I know that all's well
You're full of news and you've lots to tell

But all too soon you've got to go
There are others waiting for computers, I know
I feel so sad as we say good bye
I pray that the days will start to fly by
Its time for bed and as I climb each stair
My heart is heavy cos you're not there
Just another day over, one more has gone by
Till once again I can be with my guy
I miss you so much

IN SILENT MIND - POST TRAUMATIC STRESS DISORDER?

What does that mean? I come back from seeing things you would not believe. Sleep deprivation, senseless cruelty, mind boggling stupidity.

The constant feeling of guilt. Why him, not me? I worry constantly about the rest of the platoon/regiment.

I may have resigned and returned to civilian life but I still remember, I still have nightmares, it's always in the back of my mind.

I don't know how to explain to those nearest and dearest to me that I just cannot pick up the pieces as before.

I feel it is futile, too grasping and materialistic. I don't see the jokes any more, I don't enjoy the sport and when I see a fight in the pub or elsewhere there is one part of me that wants to shout out to stop and the other that shakes in fear remembering the gunfire and the bombs, the screams of the wounded and dying.

I want to be left alone but I am afraid of being alone.

How can you understand, do you want to understand? And if, to compound all this, I have lost a limb how can you still love me? I feel I am no longer the person I was and how can I give you and the children the life you deserve.

I snap, I sulk, I am morose. I am hyper, laugh like a maniac, I am on my own for hours on end. I hate myself because every time I do something like that I feel the guilt which turns to anger and I don't know how to get out of it.

A MILITARY WIFE

When you come home
Tired eyes, exhausted body
Heaven knows what in your mind.

I take you in my arms and hold you tight
Trying to dissolve that layer of darkness,
Separating the strands of what you
Have gone through.

I know and understand that this will be in the back
Of your mind until you regain your regiment again.

But, my darling, while I hold you in my arms
I want you to know that it's all right.

The children are so excited that you are home
They crowd around you asking so many questions,
Wanting you to join in their games.

The baby is still unsure of who you really are but
Somehow, you are recognised.

They are the best form of relaxation you can have.

When you lie by my side at night,
I am totally there for you.

The fact that repairs need to be done,
The daily grind requiring attention,
That can all wait.

Rest awhile in my arms
Let the troubles in your mind relax.

Sleep my love, you are home
Safe in my arms.

Tomorrow we go forward together.

RECIPE FOR AN ARMY WIFE

1 1/4 cup of Patience
1 tsp Courage
1 lb Adaptability
1 1/4 cup Tolerance
Dash of Adventure
Splash of Humour

Mix the ingredients with 2 tsp of elbow grease,
Leave alone for 8 months.
Marinate with tears.
Sprinkle every so often with money.
Season with international spices.
Bake for 20 years or until done.
SERVE WITH PRIDE

MY BODY IS IN NEED OF LOVE

My body is in need of love
My heart is full of pain
You have gone to war
Yet our love will always remain

Times are hard and times are rough
They will only make us tough
I will be strong and I'll survive
Knowing you will be back by my side

Months go by day by day
Everything gets hard to say
Sitting here waiting for you
The only thing I know to do

The night is dark and sometimes day too
Just remember our love is true
You be safe and dream of me
We'll be together soon, very soon,
You will see

OUR LOVE WAS YOUNG

Our love was young
Only just begun
Then you were gone
In full combat gear
Without saying goodbye

Off to war
In a land so far
Just what is it for
This pointless war?

My heart you have taken
All alone now I weep
Just your photos and memories I keep

Waiting for your calls and letters each day
I pray to the Lord to keep you safe
And bring you home to me one day

I count down the days
Until you are home with me
In my arms safely
There you will stay

A soldier you are
All big and strong
Serving your country
To keep us safe

My love for you is strong
My soldier, my man
All alone I sleep at night
Longing to be in your arms once more

WHY WOMEN CRY

A little boy asked his mother "Why are you crying?"
"Because I'm a woman" she told him.
"I don't understand" he said.
His mum just hugged him and said, "and you never will."

Later the little boy asked his father, "Why does mother seem to cry for no reason?"
"All women cry for no reason" was all his dad could say.

The little boy grew up and became a man, still wondering why women cry.

Finally he put in a call to God. When God got on the phone, he asked, "God, why do women cry so easily?"

God said, "When I made the woman she had to be special. I made her shoulders strong enough to carry the weight of the world, yet gentle enough to give comfort.
I gave her the inner strength to endure childbirth and the rejection that many times comes from her children.

I gave her a hardness that allows her to keep going when everyone else gives up, and take care of her family through sickness and fatigue without complaining. I gave her the sensitivity to love her children under all circumstances, even when her child has hurt her very badly.

I gave her strength to carry her husband through his faults and fashioned her from his rib to protect his heart. I gave her wisdom to know that a good husband never hurts his wife, but sometimes tests her strengths and her resolve to stand beside him unfalteringly.

Finally, I gave her a tear to shed. This is hers exclusively to use whenever it is needed."

"You see my son" said God, "the beauty of a woman is not in the clothes she wears, the figure she carries, or the way she combs her hair. The beauty of a woman must be seen in her eyes, because that is the doorway to her heart –

The place where love resides."

A REASON, A SEASON, A LIFETIME

People come into your life for a reason, a season or a lifetime. When you know which one it is, you will know what to do for that person.

When someone is in your life for a REASON it is usually to meet a need you have expressed. They have come to assist you through a difficulty, to provide you with guidance and support, to aid you physically, emotionally or spiritually.

They may seem like a godsend, and they are. They are there for the reason you need them to be. Then without any wrongdoing on your part, or at an inconvenient time, this person will say or do something to end the relationship. Sometimes they die. Sometimes they walk away. Sometimes they act up and force you to take a stand. What we must realise is that our need has been met, our desire fulfilled, their work is done. The prayer you sent up has been answered and now it is time to move on.

Some people come into your life for a SEASON, because your turn has come to share, grow or learn. They bring you an experience of peace, or make you laugh. They may give you something you have never done. They usually give you an unbelievable amount of joy. Believe it, it is real, but only for a season.

LIFETIME relationships teach you lifetime lessons, things you must build upon in order to have a solid emotional foundation. Your job is to accept the lesson, love the person and put what you have learned to use in all other relationships and areas of your life.

It is said that love is blind, but friendship is clairvoyant

Thank you for being a part of my life, whether you were a reason, a season or a lifetime.

A FLOWER IN THE DESERT

Through the glare of the sun
Over the rolling sand
Something catches my eye.
A flower so bright
So tall and so proud
Graces the desert sky.

It's beauty takes my breath away
So delicate yet so bold.
It really looks so out of place
Amongst the war torn fold.

Still it keeps on blooming
Its strength is clear to see.
It's courage to stand tall and proud
In a place it shouldn't be.

You wonder why it doesn't wilt
Why petals never fall.
Think determination and courage
That flower has it all.

Close your eyes and picture it
I'd like the World to see.
I'm very proud of that flower
You see that flower belongs to me.

WORTH THE TEARS

Her sadness at his leaving
Was worth a million tears
For the memories that she carries
Will see her through the years

The love he freely gave her
Had warmed her cold cold heart
Would keep the fire burning
All the time they were apart

So he smiled as he was leaving
Called her softly, 'dear'
He told her that he loved her
Though he must leave her here

For parting's such sweet sorrow
Sure she's heard the poet say
But they would meet again tomorrow
Though they were sad today.

Even though I was sad when my son went off, the happy memories I have of him when he is at home are worth the parting at the end, I think. Although he doesn't say much, he did buy me a little ornament of three baby elephants in a knitted jumper and the words on the base said "Love is a close knit family." Everyone say Ah! It was my birthday and I do like elephants, but he does not buy cards or presents not even for mother's day so this was special for me.

Thing is, I never understood men 'till I raised a son and realised that they keep all their love inside them after about the age of 14. I now know that just because love isn't shown it doesn't mean its not felt. Funny thing too, my dad (RIP) told me years ago and I never understood what he meant until I had a son!

CHILDREN

By sending letters, Xmas cards, and jokes, children help to bring some normality to our troops. It raises their morale and reminds them that we all care.

TO ALL THE TROOPS FROM A SEVEN YEAR OLD

I sometimes watch the news with my mummy and I see you on there. I hope you are ok and I am thinking of you.

REPLY....

You are a Star. We have read your e-mail in Iraq and send you a big 'Hello' from all troops.

TO A SOLDIER

I'm not sure what soldier though, 'coz there are loads of you. So I'm better saying, To a Soldier that gets the chance to read this card from a 13 year old girl that is very proud of what you are doing. So anyway I'm 13 years old, I bet I would never have the courage to do what you are doing. It must be so hard for you to be staying away for Christmas, my present to you is this letter. I know it's not much but it's all I can give you. It would be kind of funny if I could fly a McDonalds out to you though. HAHAHA

I hope you stay safe and come home to your family soon. I don't know how you can stay away so long. I couldn't do it. Anyway me and all my family are proud of you, stay strong, stay safe and you know you will becoming home soon. Well, it's 2.21 am. Better be off.

Much love

FROM THE CO (COMMANDING OFFICER)

I just wanted to take this opportunity to say thank you to all those who made the wonderful cards that we were sent over this Christmas. There was obviously a lot of effort put into the making of them and this letter of thanks is the least we can do to show our gratitude.

It is never easy to be away from home for as long as we can be, but being away at Christmas just makes the whole thing seem that little bit worse. Getting mail from home is certainly the highlight of any soldier's day giving us instant morale and this is definitely the case with anything to do with Christmas.

What made these cards so special, however, is that they were handmade by you, and that you of course have never met us before. It is extremely kind of you all to have made these cards and have them sent over to us. I would personally like to say thank you on behalf of all of the soldiers who received the cards and hope that you all had a very merry Christmas, enjoyed your New Year and are making the most of being back at school for a new term.

FROM A SOLDIER

To all the children at the junior school. Thank you very much for all your cards, it's so good to know people are thinking of us out here and all the lads loved them! It made everyone smile and everyone has their own card which they chose.

I would also like to thank all the teachers for allowing this to happen, it's amazing how little things lift morale so high. These cards are much appreciated and very special to me as they brought a piece of home with them.

So thank you, everyone, at the junior school. I hope you have a lovely Christmas and a Happy New Year!

Yours gratefully

A MEDLY OF NOTES AND JOKES SENT TO THE SOLDIERS

Dear soldier,

I am eight years old. I am writing to thank you for fighting the Taliban to free the Afghan people. It must be very hard. I hope you are doing well and the time is passing quickly. You must have a lot of guns to look after. Do you have a favourite tank? It must be fun crushing the bugs…

Best wishes

Dear soldier,

I am eight years old. I am writing this letter to thank you for all you are doing in Afghanistan. You must be very strong, brave and fierce… Afghanistan is many miles away and looks very hostile… I hope that you will be home soon with your family. We all think that soldiers are very brave trying to sort out difficult problems.

Dear Soldier,

I thought I would write to say thank you for fighting in the war for our country… I am so sorry if you are suffering… I had to suffer recently, my grandmother died a few weeks ago. I was really sad. Unfortunately she smoked. I have decided I won't smoke and I hope you don't smoke. I don't want you to die as well…

Aged 10

Dear Soldier,

I am eight years old… I want to thank you for what you are doing in Afghanistan. Do you have any time to sit down and rest? Are you missing anyone in your family? I always miss my Mummy and Daddy when I am away from them. It must be difficult for you. I hope God protects you and that with your bravery you can help to solve the problems that make one man fight another from the same country…

Dear Soldier,

In the news we see reports of the difficult job you have to do so I thought I would write and say YOU ARE DOING GREAT…

Age 10

Dear Soldier,

Guess what! Tony Blair has resigned plus the new Harry Potter book is almost out!…

Age 10

Dear Very Brave Soldier,

I am writing to tell you that I am very grateful for the very difficult job you do. I am always seeing reports on the News about an incident in Afghanistan. I think your job is one of the most important in the world – to keep peace…

Age 10

Dear Soldier,

In the news we see reports of the difficult job you have to do. I think you are very courageous and I admire your strength. I would never be able to do something so brave and I wish I could do more…

Age 13

Doctor, Doctor, I feel like a curtain…… Then pull yourself together.

What animal is the best at cricket?…… A bat!

There are two flies in a saucer playing football.
One says to the other "We'd better win next week, we are in the cup"!

FROM A SOLDIER

Hello Junior School,

Thank you for your time in making me a Christmas card. It is nice to know that someone back home is thinking of me and the boys out here in Afghanistan. I say a special thank you to year 4 as I received a card, and would like to let them know the joke on the front of the card was great and it made me and the troops around me laugh. So thank you.

I hope you all have a wonderful Christmas and get every present you wish for.

Again, many thanks to you for making me smile when I am so far from home.

On a sadder note, there are the goodbyes to the fathers who have not come home.

MY DAD

He was a great Father
For every good reason
I wish he was still alive
He would still be with me
If it hadn't gone wrong
I wish he had survived.

I feel like it was all a dream
But it's not what it seems
That he's still with me in my heart
And in my sad sad dreams.

I'm crying at this moment
But I can't stop now
I wish he was still with me
And he's whispering in the clouds.

I will visit you in your dreams
And we shall roam free
Playing in the grassy fields
Definitely you and me.

A GOOD FRIEND OF MINE

My poem for you today, is not to make you sad, nor for causing any sorrow, for you brave and grateful lads.
But lately I've been thinking, and it just won't leave my mind, how you were always there for me, a real good friend of mine.

You all died in an accident, and I know that I'm not wrong, your friendship stuck together, and that's what made you strong.

The pain it struck me hard, just like a thousand knives stabbing me over and over, they took your innocent lives.

You never done anything wrong, which makes you real good guys. Just thinking of your cheery smile bring upsetting tears to my eyes.

I'm really going to miss you, your soul will never die. You know I loved you more than life, you make me want to cry.

Now remember you had a special family, true, caring and kind. Unfortunately you had to leave them, leave them all behind.

I know you'll all be together again, one day in the sky. But for now, all I have to say is....
I'll miss you and goodbye

DAD

You fought to your end,
And you fought for us all
But we never imagined
That you would fall

You lived your life to the full
Not one day passed you by
Life and soul of the party
But now we weep and we cry

For your country and self
You did what you must
You fought for your family
Through mud, rock and dust

You won't return home
For you have no need
You fulfilled your life
And your soul has been freed

Your dreams came true
When you were alive
A gorgeous wife
And girls, beautiful all five

For they all hold a piece of you
Whatever that may be
And for that we are all
So very happy

We'll keep you in our memories
And in our hearts too
When we catch our reflection
We'll see a piece of you

Go now and be free
For your body's rest
You'll love me forever
From this world to the next

And I'll love you always
For you know
Through all my years
You've been my hero

YOU WERE LIKE A SECOND DAD

It wasn't your time, it was an accident, the plane just had to go down.
I believe there was a technical fault that threw your plane to the ground.

If only you had got on another plane you could still be with us today,
The last words I ever said to you was I'll see you another day.

But that's not going to happen, cause I'll never see you again.
You've definitely gone to a better place, you're a truly grateful friend.

I'm really going to miss you, an awful, awful lot.
The smell of your cooking tickled my nose while bubbling in the pot.

What is the world coming to, why did this have to happen?
I'm going to miss your revolting burps and your hideous way of laughing.

You meant a real big deal to me, you were like a second dad.
Like I said, you've gone to a better place and that's what makes me glad.

But at least you didn't die alone, there were quite a few others,
They must have been pretty good friends, maybe as good as brothers.

You were special guys to all of us, you did everything together.
You brave men put your lives at risk.

We will remember you forever.

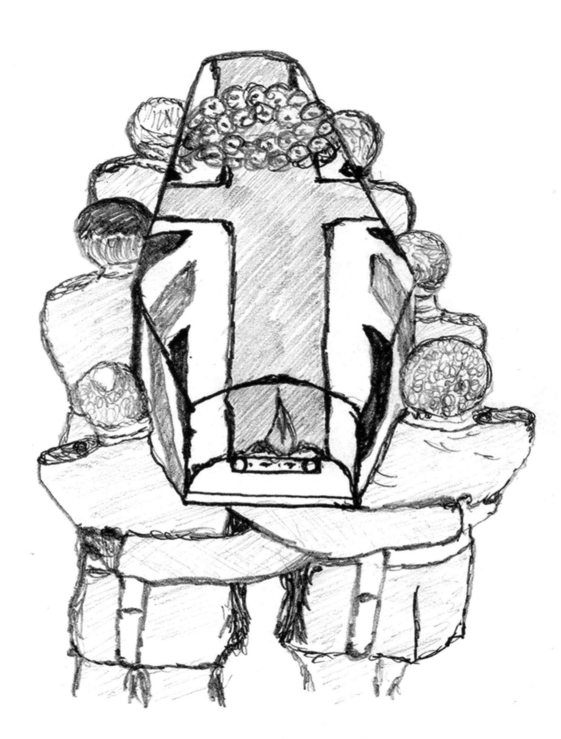

SORROW
AND LOSS

MISSING PRESUMED DEAD

I hear on the news that yet another one has died
My heart goes out to all those they have left behind
It makes me ponder on that terrifying phrase
Those three most powerful words

MISSING PRESUMED DEAD

There is a finality there, all fear is there
They have gone.
Yet one clings onto one word more than any other

MISSING.

Well, maybe they could be missing
THEY could be mistaken
You suppress any other thoughts that come into your mind
You concentrate on "could be mistaken"

You cling to that one hope you play with the words
Why "presume"? You are either dead or your are not!
Then, you know in your heart The stark, searing, pain of reality.

It's true
You'll never see them again as flesh and blood
You'll never feel them again
You'll never hold them again
You'll never hear them again

Your world has opened into this bottomless abyss
You are stabbed in the heart
You are being crushed by the weight of grief and fear

You either stay crushed or slowly start to climb out

Then when you think you have got out
You find yourself walking on the crust of another wound
Sometimes it is smooth and easy to walk on
Sometimes it is very crusty and lumpy
Other times it is so thin that you fall back in
And you start the whole process again!

The scab never heals

On and on, the process is never ending
Just longer moments in between
That is my life now

A different life started on that fateful day
One that will remain until my dying day

Not "Missing, Presumed Dead"

Just dead

Walk every moment of life's path with an open heart,
open eyes and embrace it all with open arms…

IN THE DARK

I stand alone enveloped in the dark,
I shout,
I call your name with all the longing
And yearning in my body and soul.

Emptiness, darkness, aloneness,
And then
The hint of your lips brushing my cheek.

This emptiness, darkness and aloneness
Is suddenly infused with such a deep
And profound love.
And then
It is gone.

I am standing there
Empty and alone in the dark.
A gentle breeze
Is caressing the trees.

Ah, was it the breeze?

Only I know
And I won't tell.

'TIS BETTER TO HAVE LOVED AND LOST

No man can change the course of life,
No man can blot the pain of death,
For all who loved you, left behind,
These silent words on every breath.

Our memories flood the space you left
And serve to keep you burning bright,
A life so full, a short-lived flame,
Born and passed into the light.

The life you lived, you couldn't waste,
You lived it to its greatest length,
Know now, that age can't touch your face,
Your spirit keeps its fiery strength.

You will never have to bear
The weaknesses of mortal plight,
Your soul and body, forever free,
Soaring in eternal flight.

Your strength will help those left behind
Walk bridges we have yet to cross,
When no real words will justify,
The heartache felt by your great loss.

No lines of mine, but maybe words of another,
Which hold great truth, if we stumble and fall;

'Tis better to have loved and lost
Than never to have loved at all.

Love forever,

TIME ALONE

We all need time alone after such a terrible sadness.

It was a week I needed to be on my own. To reflect, to cry and cry. How I cried! I put Frank Sinatra's "My Way" on, we were going to have that as we left the chapel. How appropriate that was. And, how I HOWLED, I SOBBED, I PLUNGED TO THE DEEPEST DEPTHS OF DESPAIR.

There is a time in the healing process that one needs to be on one's own. The pain lessens then intensifies, rather like a pulse, or the waves on the shore. At times they pound so hard at you, you can hardly breathe.

All you can do is give in gracefully to the power of that pounding and wait for the agony to subside.

And it does. The calm comes again and it's the gentle lapping on the shore. A soothing healing sensation but always tinged with the knowledge of what has been and will never be the same again.

A GODFATHER REMEMBERS

When the telephone rings before dawn my heart always sinks… I always hesitate to answer for I somehow know that something has happened to a friend or loved one.

The momentary joy of hearing a voice and the hope that all is well slowly fades… Images appear followed by sadness. Time stands still.

We have no words to comfort those that survive and as hours go by we retreat into our solitude to remember a smile, that last letter kept in the old shoebox with so many other memories.

Thankfully, no regrets of things we should have done or said… Hopefully, a prayer that the end came quickly. I shall always remember him as he was, quiet, kind and thoughtful. My last words as we embraced were "take care of yourself!". The warmth of his hug was still there as I watched him, a young man walking into an unknown future, one last glance and he was gone. As I lay in my bed remembering that moment, I was reminded that life is short and happiness fleeting.

THIS BOTTOMLESS ACHE IN MY HEART

I lie there in the morning with this bottomless ache in my heart
A piece torn out which can never be mended
There for the rest of my life
What is the point of going on, I ask
What reason to do anything

Then, I think, just a moment,
There are others who can say this with much more reason than I

And I know that I will go on, not because I must, but it is the way I AM
I am not so selfish a person as to presume that it is only me, and my
    world, that has disintegrated.
What right have I to say that

One small drop in the infinity of all
But how those ripples grow.

Without all that has gone before
Right up to your untimely death
How could we have known joy, happiness and delight
So proud of you we are

The gift you have given us of how much love there is for you
The loyalty of your friends
The respect of your peers and superiors
The love of your girl and meeting all her family
What joy that brings

These are the silver linings, my darling
In a dark and heavy place
And, slowly the light will return for all of us
A shadow of darkness will always remain
Hence the ache is always there
But ultimately more manageable.

I AM DEFINITELY TWO

Three years now have gone
As the waves come and go
So dies time
The relentless pulling and pushing
The high and the low
Sometimes pulling
Sometimes pounding
Sometimes crashing
Sometimes calm
Sunlight dancing on the waters

But I am definitely two

I am the social face
I do enjoy my friends
Being there for them and others

I am also the face you rarely see

Look deep into my eyes
And you will always find it there
Not in self pity
But in sadness of yet another loss
The loss of another life
The loss of opportunities missed
Weddings, births, the joy of
Watching your children and
Grandchildren grow.

Do you think that is morbid?
It is my pain to bear
And one which I bear
With as much grace as I can.

I am definitely two.

REMEMBERING YOU

We look at family and friends everyday
Not thinking one day they will go away
Then out of the blue their life has ended
Leaving me here undefended
Why did you go? Why can't you stay
By my side forever and a day
Now I think of you most of the time
When I'm lonely and need you by my side
Knowing you are around trying to help
Your spiritual guidance will be felt
Thank you for being with me
Sharing your life with precious memories to view
Goodbye my friend, knowing you was worthwhile
The pain will subside, the more I remember your
Smile

THE GRAVESIDE

We wander to your graveside
And place each
Flower with care,
For the Son and Brother
We love so dearly,
Is sleeping there.

If memories
Keep us together,
Then we are never
Far apart,
From early morn
To silent night
You're always in our hearts

GOODBYE BRAVE SOLDIER

Wall to wall tears in the silent, sombre Church
White faces and eerie quietness

Sobs break out as the Flag-draped coffin is carried in
Then – unbearably – a little boy cries, "Daddy!
Daddy! Wanna see Daddy!"

The soldier is remembered, his favourite music played
The entire congregation then walks together to the burial.

Townsfolk stand still and bow their heads
And watch the procession go slowly, quietly past

Brothers-in-Arms gently place their sad burden down.
Grieving but heads held high

A Gun Salute
The Last Post
Lots and lots of flowers

Goodbye, Brave Soldier – Goodbye

GONE BUT NOT FORGOTTEN

God – please help the families today of
Our young heroes who were stolen away
Numbness, heartache, grief, pain but
Eternal pride and love for them remain

Brave and selfless
Unswervingly loyal
Their names will live on

Never to be gone from
Our hearts and souls
They will not grow old

Four of the best
O God grant them rest and
Remember the ones left in sorrow
Go with them please through the valley
Of tears and shadows and grant that
Tomorrow – they may know
That their loved ones will never be gone
Ever in our memory, they will always live on
Never to be forgotten

IN MEMORY OF THE FALLEN

Look to the skies on a crystal clear night
For there spread before you is a wondrous sight
You may be wondering what's all the glory
Just hold on a minute and hear my story

On September 11 2001 America's world tore apart.
Evil was unleashed that day, it struck right at their heart

Then over to England this evil curse spread
Creating havoc and mayhem. Leaving innocents dead.
So decisions were made and tactics were planned
To stamp out this curse in its own homeland

Coalition forces deployed from land, sea and air
To rid our world of the evil hiding there

It's five years on now, there's no end in sight
While evil still lurks there we'll stand and we'll fight

And for each life that is lost a new star will be born
Shining down on earth from dusk until dawn

You see stars hold the spirits of those lives now fallen, our brave men
And women whose lives were stolen

Their memories live on in the stars up above
They're resting in peace now, still holding our love
NOW, look to the skies on a crystal clear night
You'll see spread before you
A truly wondrous sight

OLIVER'S ADVICE

I have a cunning plan he said,
But not to be known until I am dead.
No ordinary man am I,
Willing to sit in an office and look at the sky.
I crave adventure,
Challenging myself,
Push to the limits body and soul.

I found it in a holy war
Dominated by fanaticism and ideology,
Exacerbated by politicians.
I saw it all in black and white
And looked far into the dark night.
I did it so that you could all sleep safe
And stay within the light.
But then my time came with a bang!
And you all went to pieces.
I, just floated off.

I went too early that I know
And did not mean this to end so.
But here I am
Where there is no Anger, hatred, or fear
Just peace.
I am home

There will come a time when we shall meet again
I will always be there for you.
So, remember,
Whatever you do,
Do it with conviction.
Help others along the way.
Live life to the Full.

ETERNALLY NEARBY

I know you cry
Every single day
And wish I was still there
You constantly pray

I am with you
When you wake in the morn
And your heart still broken
Shattered and torn

I watch with pride
As you put on your mask
The one that gets you through
Your public task
When people ask "how are you today"
"I'm getting there" I hear you say

I still see though
When you close your door
Every emotion and hurt
Is so painfully sore

I touch your face
Help you try to regain
Your beautiful smile
Please don't be in pain

I walk with you
Into dreamland at night
I take hold of your hand
And together we take flight

I want you to know
Wherever you go or whatever you do
I am eternally nearby
Forever close to you

A YEAR TO THE DAY

A year's gone by!
Did you see it fly?
So much has been done
So many people lost and found
So many old friendships rekindled.

So much love and support
So many tears shed
So much pain in the heart
So much exhaustion
So much numbness
So much nothingness

So much strength
So much compassion
So much knowledge
So much understanding
So LITTLE understanding!
So much fear

So much pride
So much warmth in the heart
So much laughter
So much thanks to the universe

So much thanks to you mother earth

I am held by the sun
The moon and the stars
With my feet firmly on the ground
I feel the beat of the earth
The song of the birds
The breath of the trees
The gently caressing of the wind
The cleansing of the rain

I am, I am, I am

THE POWER OF
AN INKED FINGER

Iraq And Afghanistan

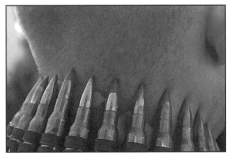 

This little ditty was written to put inside parcels.

To everyone that's in the Forces
Getting these boxes is like picking horses

Some you win....some you lose
Some you wish you didn't choose

But no matter what you find inside
It's been packed and sent with loving pride

From all of us here to you out there
We would like you to know that
WE DO CARE

OFFICE

I sit and wait for news of the team
Nothing to do but sit and dream
Thinking of my 2 weeks leave
Putting the presents under the tree

My little boy my fantastic wife
These are the people that bring joy to my life
Unwrapping presents all morning long
Sitting out here some say is wrong

Doing my job as best I will
Just been informed a life stood still
This seems all so far away
A soldier has died on a stretcher he lay

The vehicle he was in was blown to bits
It's times like this a tour is the pits
I suddenly feel pretty sick
Can't tell the boys they'll think I am tit
I really don't want to write anymore
The team are ok I am sure

A LETTER FROM THE FRONT

Just a quick note to thank you so much for the parcels you sent recently. Reaching us here this morning the lads have been tucking in since then! It was good to have some deodorant to smell normal again, not like we can go on a night out or anything, around here!

Seriously, if it was not for the humility of people like yourselves doing what you can, it means so much out here and makes our jobs that little bit easier. Not just keeping us well supplied but to know that every day people support us and what we are doing.

Sadly the battalion suffered its first casualties a few days ago for our sister company in …. Only time can help them grieve and getting back out and stuck into the job we came here to do. Paratroopers and the army are a strong breed. Nowhere else will you find the 'stiff upper lip' so voluntarily adopted in times of crisis, no greater effort to move on despite the religious remembrance of the dead. It's a brotherhood, and despite the loss of some of our family, Paras run from nothing.

Despite this seemingly dire situation, there is a lot of good being done here, the people are so different, yet so similar too. Winning their support is the key to this battle. It is a beautiful country which I pray we can bring stability to through our efforts.

So with resolute steadfastness, and with a tear in the eye, we carry on. For us here, every contact with the UK feels like home and takes us back there, just for a few minutes, every time the helicopter with post arrives. Think of it not as sending things out to help the troops, think of it as sending a small piece of home, just a few minutes of detachment from this place, to help us remember what they have got to look forward to and what they are fighting for.

Please continue to support us, as we try to support you.

A POEM SENT FROM OPS SEC IRAQ

The night before Christmas
On a quiet Iraqi patrol
Just me and a few others
Out here in the cold

The snow was falling
On this cold winter's night
When all of a sudden
There appeared a dim light

It seemed to be rising
From the East it appeared
I told all the others
To stay quiet and near

We have visitors
Either friendly or foe
We called our commander
He said to lay low

The light got brighter
And the snow slowed down
We crouched under cover
Not making a sound

Not too many people
Knew we were out here
The sound of a Chinook
Was now getting near

Lights from the chopper
Lit up all around
Then someone appeared
Repelling to the ground

With no communication
From the bird in the sky
The chopper just hovered
With its blinding lights

Then came the voice
And a jolly ho ho ho
From back in my youth
That sound I would know

We couldn't believe
The sight that was there
Dressed in a red suit
With snow white hair

His sack was full
And he had a big smile
The night was still
For a little while

That Santa with his sack
Brought Christmas to us
Out here in Iraq

FOR MY MAM

Remember me when I'm gone
Don't remember me just for my song
Remember the good times, forget the bad
Remember us and what we had

And you'll hear my whisper in the wind
You'll see my face smile in the sky
Feel my arms around you when you cry
You'll feel my shadow in your dreams
Remember us and where we'd been

Remember when it was me and you
What ever hit us we'd see it through
Forget about when I caused you grief
Turn it over and start a new leaf
Remember me as your soul mate
Remember my life, it was great

And you'll hear my voice in the rain
You'll see me shining in the stars
You'll feel me hold you when you sleep
You'll see my shadow when you weep
You have my love, it's yours to keep

Remember how we used to laugh at anything
I haven't forgotten I still wear my ring
Don't blame yourself for my pain
It washes away in the summer rain
Don't ever think it was your fault

And you'll hear me shout in a storm
And see my face in the clouds
Feel my grace in the rain
And when it goes
Feel no pain

KEEP YOUR CONDOMS IN YOUR CAR!

My wonderful girlfriend and I had been dating for over a year, and so we decided to get married. There was one little thing bothering me. It was her beautiful younger sister.

My prospective sister-in-law was twenty-two, wore very tight miniskirts, and generally was bra-less. One day my 'little sister' called and asked me to come over to check the wedding invitations.

She was alone when I arrived, and she whispered to me that she had feelings and desires for me that she couldn't overcome. She told me that she wanted to make love to me just once before I got married and committed my life to her sister.

Well, I was in total shock, and couldn't say a word.

She said, "I'm going upstairs to my bedroom and if you want one last wild fling, just come up and get me." I was stunned and frozen in shock as I watched her go up the stairs. When she reached the top she pulled off her pants and threw them down the stairs at me.

I stood there for a moment, then turned and made a beeline straight for the front door.

I opened the door and headed straight for my car. Lo and behold, my entire future family was standing outside, all clapping!

With tears in his eyes, my future father-in-law hugged me and said, "we are very happy that you have passed our little test. we couldn't ask for a better man for our daughter. Welcome to the family."

And the moral of this story is:
Always keep your condoms in you car.....hahahahah

ONE BAD SOUL

Another dusty day in the desert
I'm still hanging around, ever present
Waiting for "End Ex" to be called
In the meantime, too many are getting mauled
This country could have been so rich
Instead of living life in a ditch
One bad soul is all it takes
To put so many lives at stake
What was he thinking? I bet Hitler knows!
Leaving the population to take the blows
So we came to cleanse Babylon
We'll make it better, now the Dictator's gone
Another step in our "War on Terror"
The vicious ruler could not see his errors
Our part in the story is finished
Too many lives have diminished
We've been in this country far too long
Let's leave it to the Iraqis to sing their own song
We need to think of our own country for a start
We need to look closer to our hearts
Back home we need to take a stand
Forget Iraq what about our homeland
We have terrorist living in our towns
With the aim to bring us all down
So let us leave Iraq
And start to win our country back!

DEJA VU, IN IRAQ

The day falls into one
They all seem the same
I've been here forever
I long for English rain
It's hard to keep your sanity
When you know what's coming next
You walk around aimlessly dreaming
Feeling slightly perplexed
Friday, Monday and Tuesday
The days fall into one
The easiest way to judge time
Is with the rise and fall of the Sun
You make friends with people
Who shouldn't get a second glance
It would be a lonely six months
You need to give them a chance
Too many people I've met
Their faces blended together
Very few I will remember
Most I will never
My days here are numbered
Less then a month I'll be gone
One day to push because
The days fall into one.

GOD IS A BULLET

When will the fighting stop?
When will we leave this place?
Things are getting worse
It's starting to be a disgrace
Everyday we get attacked
I don't like it anymore
I'm wasting my short life away
Laying on these dusty floors
Too many have passed away
There will be more to come
It's time to pack our bags
Turn around and quickly run
This country's going to self destruct
We're in the firing line
Let's close this place down
It's about bloody time
Those that have passed away
Are Mothers, Fathers, Daughters, Sons
I have now seen God
He comes in the form of a gun
I still love the job I do
But I want guidance from above
Do I really want to leave my family
Without the one they love?

ANGEL IN THE DARK

The freezing cold
The dark of the night
The moon and the stars my only light
The Devil is here
He's at my side
Inviting me closer with arms open wide
I run away, I'm really tired
He's on my shoulder
There's nowhere to hide

Then I hear your voice through the night
I feel your love turn to light
It gives me my strength to fight
You are the good in my life
Because you're all that's pure
You're my angel shining in the dark
The light throughout the night

In the pouring rain he's here again
You hear my screams, you feel my pain
He reaches forward he's squeezing my heart
I look to the sky to see the clouds part

And I hear your voice releasing me
I feel your love set me free
You're the only good in my life
And you're all that's pure
You're my angel in the dark
You're my light throughout the night

Walking home he's surrounding me
There's more of him than you or me
He fills the street, the whole city
He's coming closer, it's getting tight
I try to fight back with all my might
But he's to my left and he's to my right

I'm going down I can't keep his pace
I look to the sky and I see your face
I hear your voice shielding me
And I feel your love set me free

It ends tonight
Me or him?
Let fate decide who will win

You banish him for eternity
We're living free, you and me
Me and my angel in the dark
My light throughout the night

IN A DIFFERENT ROOM

I see the same stars
I see the same moon
As it just happens
I'm in a different room

The sun still shines
The birds still tweet
It's the same old ground
Beneath our feet

My heart will never dwindle
My love will never fade
Home is where the heart is
Regardless of where I'm laid

I can see your faces
I can feel your smiles
I'm always near you
Give or take a few miles

I think the same thoughts
I feel the same gloom
I'm always with you
I'm just in a different room

IT'S CHRISTMAS DAY, ALL IS SECURE

Twas the night before Christmas
He lived all alone
In a one bedroom house
Made of plaster and stone

I had come down the chimney
With presents to give
And to see just who
In this home did live

I looked all about
A strange sight I did see
No tinsel, no presents
Not even a tree

No stocking by the mantle
Just boots filled with sand
On the wall hung pictures
Of far distant lands

With medals and badges
Awards of all kinds
A sober thought
Came through my mind

For this house was different
It was dark and dreary
I found the home of a soldier
One I could see clearly

The soldier lay sleeping
Silent, alone
Curled up on the floor
In this one bedroom home

The face was so gentle
The room in such disorder
Not how I pictured
A lone British soldier

Was this the hero
Of whom I'd just read?
Curled up on a poncho
The floor for a bed?

I realised the families
That I saw this night
Owed their lives to these soldiers
Who were willing to fight

Soon round the world
The children would play
And grownups would celebrate
A bright Christmas Day

They all enjoyed freedom
Each month of the year
Because of the soldiers
Like the one lying here

I couldn't help wonder
How many alone
On a cold Christmas Eve
In a land far from home

The very thought brought
A tear to my eye
I dropped to my knees
And started to cry

The soldier awakened
And I heard a rough voice
"Santa, don't cry,
This life Is my choice

I fight for freedom
I don't ask for more
My life is my God,
My Country, my Corps."

The soldier rolled over
And drifted to sleep
I couldn't control It
I continued to weep

I kept watch for hours
So silent and still
And we both sat and shivered
From the cold night's chill

I didn't want to leave
On that cold, dark night,
This guardian of honour,
So willing to fight

Then the soldier rolled over
With a voice, soft and pure
Whispered "carry on Santa,
It's Christmas Day, all is secure."

One look at my watch
And I knew he was right
"Merry Christmas my friend,
And to all a good night"

HELP RAISE MORALE IN AFGHANISTAN

Well, I've sent my boy out:

A catapult (for those camel spiders!)
Water bombs
An inflatable Stella bottle
Water bomb catapults
Water pistols and palm pistols (that strap to your wrists)
Mini Operation game
Table football
Finger football
Dominos
'Erotic' cards (didn't realize just how erotic until I bought them,
    all the girls have their foofs out!)
Magazines
Funky straws for blow football
Loads of mini travel games
Pirate stuff – banners, games etc 'cos all of us (me and his friends)
    went out in fancy dress as Pirates so I sent him his own pirate party
Bucket and spades
Loads of top trumps
Crossword puzzles
And a ton of other things
That I can't remember

He is leaving nearly all of that stuff
Out there when he comes back
LATER THIS MONTH

A BRITISH SOLDIER'S AFGHANISTAN POEM
(A TAKE ON A FRONTLINE SOLDIER'S VIEW
IN HELMAND PROVINCE)

Lungs full of dust, feet blistered and torn
Uniforms in shreds but with pride they are worn
Little sleep do we get and our rations are poor
So we ask the Americans and they give us more

Many miles we have trodden in this heat hot as hell
And the horrors that we witness our loved ones we don't tell
In firefights in compounds hunkered down against a wall
We do our duty with pride and pray that we won't fall

The GMLRS, Warriors and Vikings have their place here in the fight
We hope in years yet to come they're not our nightmares in the night
But we have our job to do today our orders have come through
It's yet another Helmand compound to be cleared by me and you

No more post again for a week or two nor calls can we make
Till we're back in camp for supplies again and an hour's respite we
    can take
Too frequent now IEDs our brothers lost and wounded here where
    we stand
And no time today to mourn them as we continue the fight in this
    God forsaken land

So roll on the end of tour when from hell we can depart
And two months home with loved ones that we cannot wait to start
The time will go so quickly when at home again we be
My next op tour Afghan? I will have to wait and see.

RUPERT

There is a new bloke who has tipped up late
I'd like to think I could call him a mate
He's pretty posh but down to earth
Most officers I've met are much worse

He normally comes down here for a brew
Officers like him there are far too few
This is a bloke, who is very well known
Some would say he's even close to the thrown

He sits in the office with plenty of others
We go out for a smoke and he mutters
We both have a moan about the day's events
This young officer doesn't sit on the fence

I sometimes feel sorry, for this young lad
Despite him having an amazing dad
Most of this family is always in the news
Tabloids give one sided views
Pictures comments no doubt it's all crap
He's even asked me for a baseball cap

It's not a problem I will do my best
Nothing to do with his family crest
If not for that he's a really good bloke
I better stop now.
I don't want him to gloat

OPS

You have just been told you're going out again
Into the mother of all lions dens
Food, water and weapons are ready
Moving out before your brekkie
It may take a 4 or 5 day drive
That's if we make there alive

People waiting for a free phone
Soldiers going out in their own little zone
You have written your letters home
Hearing soldiers in the distance continue to moan
Not enough armour or too much kit
We as soldiers don't like it one bit

You pack your day sack with bare minimum stuff
For the next ten days you're living rough
No washing or shaving just brushing your teeth
You're looking forward to home cooked beef
In a few hours you'll be on the road
In a vehicle carrying too much of a load

In a few hours you'll be out the gate
The soldiers the Taliban you've grown to hate
Suicide bombers and IED
I pray to my God it's them not me
None of many soldiers none of our men
Into the mother of all lions' dens

THE DC

Sangin was once a beautiful city
Now surrounded by war it's a pity
Mortars and rockets going off all the while
I find myself laid in a sandbag pile

Candles for lighting and a river for water
Oh bloody hell here comes a mortar
Laid up next to all the rubble
Another like that we'll be in trouble
The dust the debris along with the smoke
It's more than enough to make you choke

You finally get to your feet
The boss calls fast air the enemy are beat
The plane soars so very high
The vapour it leaves is so very fine

The rockets leave the wings so fast
Before you know it you see the blast
Taliban now are dead and gone
You try to think of a cheery song
Nothing really comes to mind
You hear the shout we have a blind

You cordon the area and call EOD
You know they'll be there in an hour or three
You lay and wait till they arrive
You think of your families and saying goodbye
All too much time on your hands
Looking forward to home with the military bands

REGAY 1

I shot this one guy in the face,
It only helps he was a nutcase
Through the branches of the tree,
The Taliban soldier falls onto his knees

From the magazine and into the breech
The tree he was using looked like beech
I spy on him using my rifle scope
X4 magnifications he had no hope

He was shooting here and there in a mad despair
My bullets hit home his face beyond repair.
I had no choice it was the only way
This is how we soldiers earn our pay.
One of the team has also been shot
The medics run over to make the blood clot
We all then move behind a wall,
The bombs are coming arranged by Paul

The dust the debris scatter all over the place
The country we fight in is a fucking disgrace
As we move to the HLS
We come under fire from over the crest

This time I have 7 62
1800 rounds so more than a few
A bullet flies past and misses by an inch
I didn't have time even to flinch

My lead wall goes into the house
Nothing could escape, not even a mouse
The Browning goes off right next to my ear
We round a corner and we are in the clear

THE TOWN

This is a place you love to hate
Welcome to Garesk it says on the gate
Over the bridge that crosses the river
A Muslim country that won't ruin your liver

Through the place they call the bazaar
It certainly is for us from afar
Both sides of the road they set up shop
This is a place we do not stop
Too many people want to meet thy God
A child looks hungry, the poor little sod

Nothing to do, but work with his dad
Going home to a mud hut, we'd call a pad
I bet you could buy almost anything here
As long as it wasn't alcoholic beer
Bottle of fanta, cooking in the sun
A mouthful of that Oh what fun

Past a garage, on the right hand side
The river is flowing along with the tide
Past a place we call Dick
Put your foot down you bloody prick
Some local in the middle of the road
Dodging cars like a fat toad
Moving past traffic craning his neck
Slowing down Oh fucking heck

Pistol drawn always ready
If you take aim you're breathing steady
It's all part of the training you've done
Locals walk past dressed like Attila the Hun

Next we come to the Hesco walls
The police lazing round the silly fools
Driving round in new 4x4s
All bought and paid for by some EU laws
This is a place we call Afghan
The bloke at the top is not a bad man
The rest all seem crooked and bent
We are the guys our government sent
This is the place we are all on tour
It's better than exercise
Oh what a bore

ALL ALONE

Walking round our deserted camp
Once again I'm dressed as a tramp
Combat trousers a green sweater
Getting home there's nothing better

I only have seven days to do
Like an animal at Chessington zoo
We all really want to just get home
And get the fuck out of the green zone

Not many people left in Shorabak
This is a place some technology lack
We all have power and the odd TV
Not washing yours hands could cause TB

Going to use the phones can seem such a chore
Walking over the stony cobbled floor
It's pretty warm and dry in the day
You can sweat just keeping the flies at bay

The nights seem so long and cold
Some soldiers in T shirts still very bold
The radio on it's the only channel you get
BFBS is always preset

Many write home at the end of each night
Up early today to watch Hatton fight
Ross on leave and John too
Leaving on camp far too few

The ops room is buzzing most of the night
The battle group deployed to take on the fight
They left last week earlier doors
The plan we think had no such flaws

Musa Qala is the main objective
The plan is fool proof it's quiet deceptive
Heliborn troops drop into the town
The 1 and 2 companies moving around
The 3 block off all the routes
If the Taliban come the soldier will shoot

Now I think its time for a shower and bed
As climb into my mossy proof shed
It really is just a tent inner
Looking forward to a home cooked dinner

2 YORKS

Sharing this room with 35 others
By the end of the tour we'd be like brothers
Arty, Reme and a Loggie troop
We all come under the Yorks battle group

The size of the bed space is very small
The bloke at the end from Liverpool
Not enough room to swing a cat
It really is as simple as that

The infantry lads spend little time here
All in the same boat not allowed a beer
The chefs all do a fantastic job
Cooking for a pretty rowdy mob

The QM boys see to our equipment needs
The padre helps with rosary beads
We have a service on a Sunday night
We also get the occasional fight

Any uncontrolled aggression and anger
Will only put our lives in danger
Medics see to all the injuries
From gunshot wounds to bleeding knees

The Det inks help bringing the news
They help us rewrite our editorial views
The buzzard in charge of all the flights
He some times plays the bugle at night

The bleeps help with all the comms
Often enough these go wrong
We also have our own MT
A Capt a Sgt plus another 3

How can I forget the sappers
They build all sorts and go like the clappers
Then we have the CQs
Some of them have very strong views
They issue kit all of the time
But some of the demands they draw the line

CO's tac goes on most of the ops
Mainly made up of bits and bobs
We also have a Qmsi
Whose level of fitness is extremely high?

Last but not least we have our own g4
The job is to get kit out the door
To fly it or drive are the only routes
From petrol ammo food and boots

I am sorry if your job I missed
I haven't got a complete list

ANOTHER DAY OUT HERE

Get up get out of bed
Scrape my face for the day ahead
Walk down the hall to the canteen
Not one day is the same routine
Booking out at the ops room
Civi cleaners pushing a broom
Empty bins and clean our sinks
It's not their fault the place still stinks

Walking to work for 9 o'clock
The ANA are in for a shock
All the soldiers are still in bed
I explain no training they are as good as dead
They get to their feet and wet their hair
Same old Afghans they do not care

Without a terp this is no good backing into a corner looking a burk,
Their Sgt enters ranting in Dari I think to myself cor fucking blimey
I cannot understand what he is saying my mind wanders off to my
    next lie in

Soldiers walking slowly to work
When they arrive the majority will shirk
Training shoes and football tops
They are in desperate need of an awful lot
Helmets shirts gloves too
The majority walk past in civilian shoes
They sit and smoke most of the day
The ones that do work get little pay
We try to explain and then we reason
But most of the day they will just not listen.
Commander, Commander you're an hour late
his bloody bloke thinks I'm his mate
He is lazy and idle thinks of no one else
No 1 priority is he himself

Can we get some trucks for the mission?
It's like asking him for a first edition
No tools or help will he give
Like putting sand into a sieve
Commander, Commander what can I do
But sit on my arse and take a pew
Getting in the cab to move a truck
It does not start, just my luck
Climb in the back to check the load
The afghan soldiers stand and goad
Tajiman, tajiman what do they say
You British soldiers get too much pay
Your Pepsi cola and your western ways
Even the amount your girls get laid.

LOST IN IRAQ

With thousands of soldiers stood at my side
I feel all alone with nowhere to hide
The feeling of despair cuts like a knife
The one thing I've learnt is to appreciate life
The soldiers at my side I know not their name
Creed, colour, religion, we are all the same
We all want to go home, I know I do
But we are here till the end to see it through
Is the War in Iraq morally right?
No questions asked our chosen job is to fight
I'm missing my wife, my boys, my folks
And sitting with friends sharing drinks and jokes
I doubt I'll come to the end of my days
But this so called God moves in mysterious ways
On my shoulders St Christopher does rest
I'm currently facing my toughest test
My morals and faith are pushed all the way
I know the good of man will shine though this day
I yearn for the day I get to go back
But for this moment, I'm lost in Iraq

THE HELMAND

Driving through the Helmand wearing your vest
Looking forward to the boss calling a rest
With top cover and Commander in tow
The morale of the boys is never low

Bouncing and stopping all to much
Included in the convoy are some of the Dutch
Top cover is constantly scanning the ground
There are never many people around
The children they call in their Pashto tongue
Young soldier's thinking of the next parcel from mum

Commander is always checking his map
All screwed up sat on his lap
There is not much room in here
For us three soldiers a terp and our gear

Ammo and water are the main issues
Top left pocket the toilet tissues
Food is easy it's boil in the bag
Been waiting 2 hours to have a lag
Keep travelling at 10k an hour
God I look forward to having a shower

The dust and the sand get in your face
Leave you with a nasty taste
We continue along the desert route
Cocooned in our armoured suits

Velcro rubbing our exposed skin
Looking forward to throwing the kit in the bin
Through the wadi and out the other end
Not knowing what's around the bend

Taliban or not I cannot tell
We only hope, they go to hell
Stop for a while checking all around
None of us move more than a bound
Check all around the wheels
Listing to soldiers doing the deals
Burger and beans for corn beef hash
No way mate I hate that gash

Fall asleep weapon by the side
Nowhere to run nowhere to hide
Awoken when someone kicks my feet
Fuck me mate I still feel beat
Off we trot once again
When we fight it's not in vain

Poem, written on an Afghan fob wall

LONELY SOLDIER

Balaclava home from home
With hesco walls and thunder domes,
A desert rose for a p***
A curried goat that did the trick!
Full of meat, the men are now,
As we hear another round.
Is it burst, or single shot
As we come under full contact.
Ricochet overhead, bury into besco sack.
What's that distant sound I hear,
My family, friends I love so dear.
No time for that, no time for tears
I must fight and beat my fears.
Side by side were standing tall
For love and peace, not for war
Heart so heavy, full of pain
I want to see my family again

THE BOSS AND THE BUILDER

Me, H and Ross driving through the night
The wind coming at you really gives you a bite
H on the gun behind on top
Ross on my left, with me in a strop

The air is clear the full moon in the sky
Driving past the poppies that are used to get high
Opium out here is the main source
This determines our action or course
We cannot just burn the lot
Although it would make an amazing phot

30 odd vehicles are way out front
The wind that hits is cold and blunt
I sit all hunched up at the wheel
The Afghan government has got a good deal

Driving up all this way on this OP
Ross tells me Kabul has a NAFFI bop
Beer and spirits what you can buy
Sorry captain I think that's a lie

The dust doesn't have time to settle
Nothing out here not a stinging nettle
The sun comes up from behind the hill
Thank fuck man I need to chill
Been driving for far to long
Been tempted to hit the Afghan bong

We manage to get a few hours sleep
Before a game called spoof I teach
The Afghan soldiers think it fun
The problem they had none of them won

As we set off there's a bang and rattle
The Taliban getting ready for battle
The tanker is what they want to hit
This is the stuff I don't like one bit
I sink down low in my seat
Dipping the clutch using me feet
All my body and muscles spasm
Nobody knows what's going to happen
For some strange reason we take a different route
Thank fuck for that I could not shoot
Feeling so open with all these trucks
The last thing you want is to get into a ruck

SATURDAY NIGHT

It's Saturday night what can I do
I'm not allowed to ring to speak to you
Can't use the computers the net is down
Drinking strong coffee a real dark brown

I miss you both it really does suck
7 years left with a bit of luck
Not long now till I'm at home
Then no need to be using a hone

I know it works out only ten days
Just being with you I'll be in a daze
It will be so much fun being home
Wish we could fly some where like Rome

The little man has grown up so fast
3 months was the time I saw him last
Before his birthday and Halloween
If it carries on like this he'll soon be a teen

Our little boy I bet he's trouble
I'll kick his arse and make him double
It's only a week till I'm home
Fed up with living in this poxy dome

Looking forward to a nice glass of wine
Go out for the night just to dine
To walk and talk with my gorgeous wife
You have given me the perfect life xxxxx

**Priscilla Dicketts** was born in the Crown Colony of Penang (as it was then) in 1948 where her Polish Father had been posted after the end of the Second World War. He later joined the World Health Organisation and Priscilla spent the first 12 years of her life living around the world. The countries she spent time in included Afghanistan, Lebanon, Canada and the Philippines. In the early 1960s her parents built a house in France just across the border from Geneva and her life became a little more settled.

Most of her senior education took place in Switzerland and she is bilingual. In 1971 she spent nearly two years working in London but returned to France vowing never to return or marry an Englishman. In 1974, in England, she married Robert and consoled herself that as he was half Hungarian this did not count!

Their only child, Oliver, was born in 1979 and whilst he grew up she ran the house and looked after the family. However, during that time, she trained as a bereavement councillor for Hospice in the Weald and worked with them for five years. She then studied Buddhism and healing.

Following Oliver's death in the Nimrod Accident in Afghanistan in 2006 and the very public interest that followed she decided with the help of some friends to try to help the Armed Forces and make the public more aware of the sacrifice that many are making. She very much hopes that by buying and reading this book the reader will gain a little insight into to the love and anguish that is part of the everyday life of members of the Armed Forces and their families.

www.priscilladicketts.co.uk

As we approach the centenary of the Great War, many of us may return to the rich legacy of war poetry from the last century and ponder Wilfred Owen's lines: 'My subject is war and the pity of war. The poetry is in the pity [...] All a poet can do today is to warn'. Sadly today, our world remains profoundly a place of conflict. While the scale of these wars can not match those of the last century, they are no less bloody, terrifying or shocking for the soldiers who fight and for the families who wait at home. Dark Clouds and Silver Linings is a collection of poems and prose filled with authentic, urgent and humbling voices responding to the myriad emotions and passions that war engenders - fear, loss, loneliness, anger, isolation and comradeship. This collection, lovingly collated by Priscilla Dicketts, is a stark reminder that we still need to be warned by poets, and that the pity of war bears repetition.

Colonel Simon Marr MBE, Royal College of Defence Studies

Nobody who reads this collection of writings can fail to be moved by them. They are a powerful evocation of the courage, human warmth, love, dignified grief and, sometimes, justifiable anger displayed by our servicemen and servicewomen, their families and friends. "Dark Clouds and Silver Linings" should be required reading for our politicians and civil servants, many of whom are lamentably disconnected from the armed forces who put their lives on the line to defend our security and freedom.

Nicholas Phillips, Bruxelles

We received a copy of your book this morning and once our son had gone to bed, I started to read it, whilst watching the X Factor, something I really look forward to on a Saturday night when my husband is away as he isn't a huge fan of reality TV. But I didn't hear a thing for the entire programme, or look up from the book once! I spent most of the time in tears and even had a bit of laughter.

Far too much in the book, I relate to, both as a wife of a soldier who, since I have known him, has spent far more time in war zones, than out of them, but also as a mother of a 4 year old boy, who says he wants to grow up and be a superhero like his dad, and join the army. I have such mixed feelings, it is hard enough to put on that brave smile waving your husband off to war, but no idea how people cope when it is your son. And your book reflects that in so many poems and stories.

I am ex RAF and I know the fantastic opportunities available, the lifelong friendships you build, the achievements, the sense of adventure you get from opportunities not available outside of the Forces and of course the sense of pride. I would be so very proud to say my son had joined any of the Armed Forces, but also a part of me would want to put my arms round him and never let him out the door.

I do know myself that I would rather have lived a very full short life, than a very long unfulfilling one and guess this is how I need to think about my sons life. I actually just wanted to write you a short message to say what a fantastic idea you had to get this book published and I think the name speaks a thousand words. And out of the dark clouds, that you live with every moment of every day, you have created something so wonderful and will benefit so many people.

I am feeling very emotional having just put the book down but also very lucky that my husband and son are ok, and all I want to do right now is tell everyone how much I love and appreciate them. When you read something like this, is puts everything into perspective and the only thing that really matters in life, are that all our loved ones are fit and well and the silly things we get all worked up about in a routine day just aren't important.

I think all of us connected to the military, feel the loss when we hear another life has been lost, or soldier has been wounded, we are all so grateful it isn't our loved ones name, but also feel so much for the people that have been left behind, parents, children, wives, grandparents etc etc. And I think you book makes us feel like we are all part of the 'Armed Forces' family.

You have created something that will live forever as well as raising money for such a worthy cause, because any one of our men and woman could find themselves needing that support one day.

A proud army wife and mother